SPRAYS OF SALT

John and Josephine Downs

Three of John and Josephine Downs' daughters: Viola Gagnon, Gladys Bedard, and Pearl Tucker, 1984. Photographs from family collection.

SPRAYS OF SALT
Reminiscences of a Native Shoaler

BY JOHN W. DOWNS

Foreword by Gayle Patch Kadlik

Gayle Patch Kadlik

PETER E. RANDALL PUBLISHER
Portsmouth, NH
1997

Peter E. Randall Publisher
Box 4726, Portsmouth, NH 03802

ISBN 0-914339-59-1

to
my favorite *Smutty Nose Rangers*—
my husband, John,
and my sons,
John, James and Christian;

to
my Uncle Buddy, Lewis A. Bedard, Jr.,
for his encouragement through the years;

and to
my dear mother,
Mrs. Gladys J. Mathieu,
whom I love with all my heart

FOREWORD

WHEN I listen to my mother reminisce about her grand-father, John William Downs, I sorely wish I had had the opportunity to know him. She uses phrases like "quiet, wonderful person," "most devoted husband," and "proud of him as my grandfather." She describes him as slender, yet strongly built, with a rugged, weatherbeaten face and a far-away look, as though often in deep thought. His character reminded her of Abraham Lincoln; and his dear wife, Josephine, of a duchess, so regal-like did she sit, quietly in her chair.

My mother refers to a weekend spent lobstering with Grandpa and helping out in his little store as "heaven!" How I long to have spent time on the water with him, to have absorbed his oneness with the sea and the Shoals, and have savored those "lobster feasts," lovingly harvested by his unfailing hard work.

John William Downs has begotten many a Shoals-lover. Many of his descendants retain more than a passing interest in the Isles of Shoals. My own family continues the Shoals tradition in our work as Smutty Nose Rangers and Isles of Shoals Historical and Research Association (ISHRA) members.

With today's increasing interest in the Isles of Shoals, it seemed appropriate to resurrect my great-grandfather's rare account of life on the Shoals. After all, he was so eloquent in his writing of it . . .

"These are some of the whispers floating from the windward side that breeze through my mind. Whispers of the times that were . . ."
John W. Downs

Gayle Patch Kadlik
Fitzwilliam, NH
March 1997

JOHN DOWNS, HARBORMASTER, DIES AT PARTY

John W. Downs, Portsmouth harbormaster, died suddenly last night at the age of 75. Stricken at the Hotel Rockingham, where he was attending a reception for navy officers here, he was rushed to the Portsmouth hospital where he was pronounced dead upon arrival. Death was due to a paralytic stroke.

Mr. Downs was born in Portsmouth but moved with his parents to the Isles of Shoals when only 10 days old and remained there until he was 14. He resided in the house where the famed Wagner murders were committed and later lived in the Wentworth-Gardner house.

His father, Ephram Henry Downs, was active in Gosport affairs before the time that the town gave up its charter and became a part of Rye.

Mr. Downs had followed the sea all his life and engaged in the lobster business during later years. During the attempts to salvage the submarine *Squalus*, now the USS *Sailfish*, his knowledge was sought by naval officials and as he explained the details of the ocean bed he gave his opinion of the possibility of a salvage method which was adopted and proved successful.

For 27 years the harbormaster, he was a member of the Portsmouth fire department and served as assistant engineer. He also was a member of the old Board of Aldermen and the city council.

Mr. Downs is survived by eight daughters, Mrs. Florence Baker of Rochester, N.Y., Mrs. Dorothy Tatum of Norfolk, Va., Mrs. Olive Moll of Alameda, Calif., Mrs. Viola Gagnon of Union, Mrs. Gladys Bedard of Dedham, Mass., Mrs. Helen

Nelson, Mrs. Pearl Tucker, and Mrs. Josephine Craven of this city; four sons: Roscoe W., Theodore R., and John B. Downs, all of Portsmouth, and Kenneth Downs of Dover; two brothers, Alex Downs of this city and Oren Downs of Boston, Mass. There are also 43 grandchildren; 15 great grandchildren and one great great grandchild.

Portsmouth Herald, October 27, 1945

JOHN W. DOWNS

Funeral services for John W. Downs were conducted yesterday afternoon by the Rev. Robert H. Dunn, rector of St. John's church at Buckminster chapel and at the grave in the family lot in Harmony Grove Cemetery.

The city was represented at the services by Mayor Mary C. Dondero, the fire department by Chief George T. Cogan, the board of registrars by John H. Yeaton.

As the funeral cortege passed the Central Fire station, several pieces of apparatus were drawn up in a line in front of the station as a tribute to Mr. Downs who for many years was a member of the department.

The bearers, all members of the department, were Herman G. Crompton, Leland W. Davis, Frank E. Amazeen, and William Palfrey.

John W. Downs

Smutty Nose Island

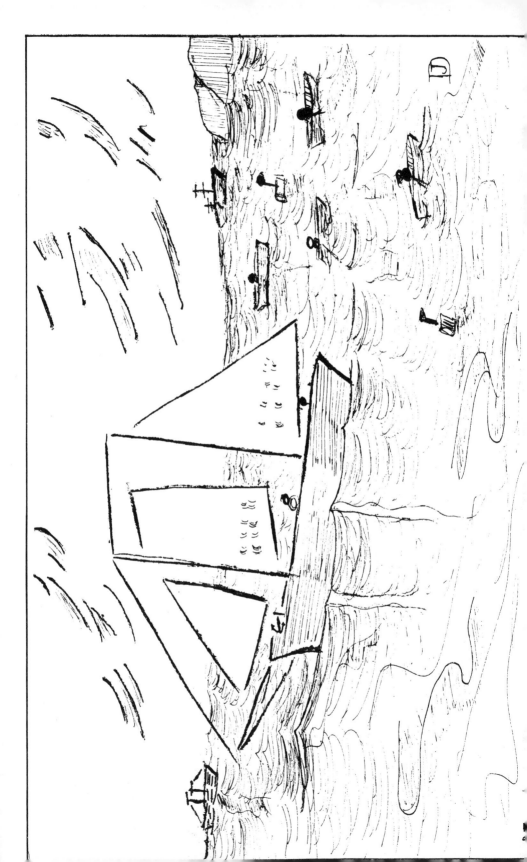

Albert Woodbury

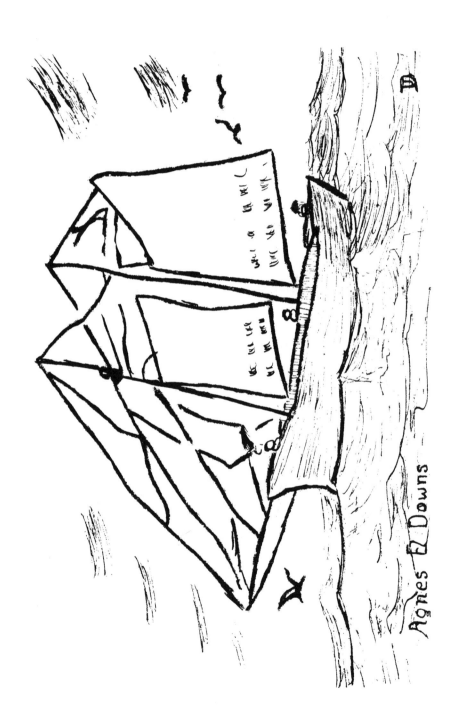

Agnes E. Downs

Helena

Foss Branch Genealogy
1-John (?-1699)
2-Joshua m. Sarah Wallis (1723)
3-Job m. Sarah Lang (1750)
4-John (1757) m. Sarah Tucker (1783)
5-Job (1785) m. Patty Berry (1809)
6-Olive Foss m. John Bragg Downs (1834)
7-Ephraim H. Downs m. Mary B. Caswell (1898)
8-John W. Downs (1870) ?

Downs Genealogy
Edward Downs
Henry Downs m. Abigail Bragg (1793)
John Bragg m. Olive Foss (1834)
Ephraim Henry m. Mary B. Caswell (1862)
Children
Henry Orrin--Edward Sargent--Mary Elizabeth--John William--
Jennie May--Florence--Alexander Foss--Arthur Merton--George

Odiorne Genealogy
1-John (1627-1707)
2-John (1675)
3-John (died 1780)
4-Benjamin m. Mary Beck (1745)
5-Benjamin (1777) m. Hannah Moulton
6-Ann Merry m. Horace Stacy Spinney (1859)
7-Horace Stacey Spinney m. Dorothy Ordiorne
8-Josephine Spinney m. John W. Downs (1889)

Sprays of Salt

BY

JOHN W. DOWNS

Compilation by Ida L. Batchelder

Printed in U. S. A.

PREFACE

I wanted with all my heart to someday write out the story of my life on the sea. Why shouldn't I? My life has been the sea, and the sea has been my life.

My story has been written from the dictates of my heart. This is no log book—as flashes of memory have recalled the incidents, I have jotted them down.

Many stories have been written about the Isles Of Shoals. Mine is to be a series of recollections—"Sprays Of Salt." I played on the rocks, an unrealizing child, as the poets and artists worked talents about me. The ocean they praised and painted was the ocean I owned and for over seventy years this ocean owned me.

I have rolled up and down on the waves of life. I have met people, some good and some bad; I have seen adventures on the sea that would make your hair stand straight; I have rowed through wealth and depression; and I have gloried in the ultimate beauty of Nature which has so often been vividly painted for me on the roof of the ocean.

My earnest prayer has been to leave an everlasting picture of life on the ocean and to prepare for the future lovers of the sea a true account, simple in content and rich in morale.

John W. Downs
479 Marcy Street
Portsmouth, N. H.

CONTENTS

SEA FEVER

"I must go down to the seas again, to the lonely sea and the
   sky,
And all I ask is a tall ship and a star to steer her by,
And the wheel's kick and the wind's song and the white sail's
   shaking,
And a grey mist on the sea's face and a grey dawn breaking.

I must go down to the seas again, for the call of the running
   tide
Is a wild call and a clear call that may not be denied;
And all I ask is a windy day with the white clouds flying,
And the flung spray and the blown spume, and the sea gulls
   crying.

I must go down to the seas again to the vagrant gypsy life,
To the gull's way and the whale's way where the wind's like
   a whetted knife;
And all I ask is a merry yarn from a laughing fellow-rover,
And a quiet sleep and a sweet dream when the long trick's
   over."

—John Masefield

CHAPTER I

THE SALT breezes sailed me right into the lap of the sea. It must have been the old god Neptune who touched my forehead with his mighty trident, the hand of fate or life's strange mystery which planted me, unbeknown, near the shores of the Piscataqua River in Portsmouth, New Hampshire.

Portsmouth has been the home of many famous persons who were born here and who have worked here to the best of their advantage in their life's work. Wafted as I was, into the midst of these surroundings, I naturally turned my attention more than once to the expressions of their views on life. On the same street, as I was born, just a few houses away on 61 Court Street, was the home of Thomas Bailey Aldrich, who wrote his life's story in the noted: "Story Of A Bad Boy" and in the same room was born Albert Laighton, the poet, a cousin of Celia Thaxter, who wrote in a style very like that of his cousin an ode of welcome for the Sons and Daughters of Portsmouth on their return home in 1873 and 1883, and who honored the name of Portsmouth in a publication of verses written by natives of the City. These two prominent men were among the many who graced the streets of Portsmouth with their idealistic temperaments.

They were two of many figures, some quaint, some historical, and many of the common ordinary who sauntered casually up and down, from time to time, along these narrow streets of Portsmouth since 1870. Looking back now, after having reached the age of seventy-two, upon the year 1870, I find that times were not so different than they are today. Europe was boiling its cauldron of war; France was battling with Prussia trying to maintain her territorial rights while the United States was beginning to build up her industries after the depression following the Civil War under the leadership of President Ulysses S. Grant and was as ever debating over the European issues of battle whenever news arrived from over seas. At that time Portsmouth was a rapidly developing fishing and trading port with a population of 9,211 people and it was I who increased this number by being born.

Outside of my mother, the most thoroughly excited member of the City at my birth, was my father. He twisted his southwester around and about, stroked his goatee nervously from time to time as he strode up and down the low-posted room, jarring the floor with his large fishing boots, uttering proverbial ejaculations of a true sea captain when there is cause for alarm. Suddenly his face began to beam and his eyes to twinkle, as the door opened and a woman, presumingly the midwife, jubilantly burst out with a tired, careworn voice:

"She's all right, Henry. It's a boy."

This was how I was launched on the fourth of January in 1870 at 56 Court Street in Portsmouth. I was christened John William Downs, the combination coupling of the two first names of my grandfathers, John Downs and William Caswell. Then, there were no records tied up in blue ribbons as to how much I weighed, when I uttered my first word, or when I took my first step. Those were minor details to be mentioned when noticed and forgotten. But it is known that twelve days after my coming into the world, my father wrapped me up in thick blankets and oilskin, encased me dutifully within his strong arms and carried me out to sea in his fishing boat. Carefully guarded from the biting sharp winds of the winter's cold, I was landed on the Isles of Shoals at the Town of Gosport. Out of the three hundred persons then living on the Island, only several must have been able to greet my father at the rudely made wharf, to see his newest pride and joy. These several, however, welcomed me on embarking from my first real sea voyage—I couldn't distinguish their faces with my newly made eyes but I could feel the warmth of friendliness from their rough and kind hearts.

Thus, I was brought out to the sea to be brought up on the sea, a born fishing man, feeling the sprays of the waves as I stretched out my baby arms to envelop the whole future in the nets of fortune.

CHAPTER II

PORTSMOUTH is just teeming with early connections of American History. Situated as it is on the south bank of the Piscataqua River and being an essential port of entry to the United States, it was early an asset to historical folklore. Famous homes of famous statesmen abound among the narrow twisted streets, and mementoes of visits of the early colonial officials have been bought by museums of art for exhibition. Benjamin Franklin placed his first lightning rod here on the home of Captain Archibald MacPhaedris, one of the finest examples of early eighteenth century architecture, and John Paul Jones lived at the Lord House on State Street while he was fitting out the "Ranger" in 1777, just before he was fully recognized as the rightful father of the United States Navy. The "Ranger" was the first ship to carry the stars and stripes officially and was built here at Portsmouth for the American Congress in 1777. Old colonial doorways are still standing and the old colonial mansions with their sea spying tops dominate the view of practically every old street in Portsmouth.

Portsmouth was settled in 1623 under the auspices of the Laconia Company. It was first called Strawberry Bank because of the unusually large strawberries found along the bank at the time of the ships' arrival. Later in 1653 it was called Portsmouth and it was incorporated as a city in 1840. It was the capital of New Hampshire, being a necessary and recognized seaport near to the coast of England from which could be sent new settlers and the required foodstuffs and armaments necessary for the proper supervision of the parties of England, until 1807, when through the coercion of prominent political parties the State capital was moved to Concord further inland. In 1897 the figures given for the population were as follows: "9,738 in 1850, 9,211 in 1870, and 9,690 in 1880." At that time even Portsmouth was "quiet and old-fashioned beyond most of the New England cities, with shaded streets and many quaint antique houses, survivals from colonial times" and was a famous summer resort.

William Brewster writes in his "Rambles About Portsmouth" of State Street, one of the stately streets of Portsmouth: "This street was the first to be furnished with paved sidewalks, and here was the place of promenade of the elite of the town. There were continual arrivals at the Piers, of ships, brigs, and schooners; and through this street there were more goods transported through it than any other in Portsmouth. Then the commerce of our merchants was extended to Europe, South America, and the East and West Indies. We find that in 1800, no less than twenty-eight ships, forty-seven brigs, ten schooners and one bark were employed on foreign voyages, belonging to Portsmouth. Seventeen of these vessels were built here in the year 1800. Twenty coasting vessels were also employed."

Over fifty years ago as yesterday I remember along the waterfront, the busy concerns occupied with their fishing business and trading with the varied types of fishermen who would come off of these foreign boats. It was generally a tumult of husky tongues and ruddy skins carrying their goods in to be traded and tasting with relish the fresh home cooked food and drinking lustily of cool beer. They were a hardy lot, tall, straight, and sunburned, typical features of the Nordic race, rushing pell-mell here and there along the water front and their first stop would usually be at the Portsmouth Brewery with its famous Bock Beer, next to the old navy yard landing.

The water front was just one of the busiest places with people coming and going from and to everywhere. At that time the land along the wharf was owned by the government. Many were the famous old landmarks of business and as I think of them, John Brouchton's lumber yard comes first to my mind as it was one of the largest that provided the lumber for the building of boats to large sailing vessels. Then there was C. E. Walker's coal wharf, Philbrick's stone shed and coal wharf; and then came good old Jo Amazeen's who kept a wholesale and retail store which used to contain anything and everything from West India rum to molasses. Commercial wharf was one of the busiest places for six months of the year, from Fall to Spring, for the big codfish were landed there. E. Jamerson and Elvin Newton and Dan Clark were the three most important fish buyers doing business in this one big extensive building. Elvin Newton was noted as one of the biggest fish buyers in New England, who would ship large cargoes to Canada and travel there with them. His famous saying was: "Live and let live." He was one grand old man. Dan Downs and Sullivan kept a lobster wharf where they boiled hundreds of lobsters. At Morris Trickert's wharf there were the salt fish dealers with its blocks of salt fish. This was managed later on by Randall and Caswell. At the end of the wharf was John Nixon's place, later owned by George Hulburt. Next came the Russell and Odiorne coal wharf which was an all land wharf close to the old library bridge and its water which used to fill the pullock dock where on the road was the old apple bakery and Sullison's smoke house where everyone would smoke hundreds and hundreds of herrings. Going down the wharf lane one would come to the merchant store of the old Jonar shop which was managed by Josisa Stockpole. There was the old foundry wharf where at one time there was a large iron foundry; the old wharf too, where the logs were boarded for the city water and the place where there was a huge water tank which supplied the steamers up river with water.

The Drowns boating wharf was always popular in those days. Mrs. Drowns used to let boats of all makes out to fishermen and parties. It was where the big yacht, "Valiant," was built by Charles Drowns. The "Valiant" was a beauty and a great sailor. I was one of the crew on her who went down to the Maine Shipyards. The last ship to be repaired there was the master "Active"—a big two master and one of the biggest two masters afloat.

Going over to New Castle along the water front, you go over the first bridge to Doane's salt fish firm which had one of the best fleet of Bankers—huge sailing vessels that used to go to the Grand Banks in the spring and always came back loaded to the brim with large codfish. At New Castle in those days, there were all fishing establishments where they owned nine vessels—all Newell's own—and mastered by Sal White and George Willard of Portland, Maine, for years and which were all moored near New Castle with many other small crafts.

Back of Water Street hundreds of men would come in to shore in fishing vessels. There would be about thirty vessels from all along the coast in and out every day and which landed thousands of pounds of fish daily as each vessel had from ten to twenty men on board. There was no power in those days to get up and down the river so they had to go with the tide; if they got going with the tide running out, they would have to row back to town two miles up river in a dory or small boat. It was some task, taking plenty of muscular strength and duration of patience. Portsmouth had some nice vessels of its own. There was the "Mary S. Hontvet"—a Grand Banker which went to the Banks for months and came home loaded with fish—the "Albert Woodbury" of Ephraim H. Downs and the "Agnes E. Downs" captained by Levi Downs, were among some of them.

Portsmouth was famous then, as it is today, for the United States Navy Yard which although located in Kittery, Maine, is more frequently termed the Portsmouth Navy Yard. Today, in 1943, extensive defense work in the secretive manufacture of submarine craft is being carried out in efficient and carefully supervised manner, and employs, at the present, nine thousand workers with a new three million dollar dry dock which eight hundred men are now building that will make it probably "the largest sub construction center in the wide world." At about 1870, it was saddened by the death of Admiral David G. Farragut who was living and had made his home within the Navy Yard. Then it was proud of its exceptionally well-balanced dry dock, 350 ft. by 105 ft., where the great war vessels of the early eighties were built.

At the Navy Yard doors, or rather to the Island Seavey, across from the doors of the Navy Yard, came the prisoners of the Spanish American War in 1897. I remember watching the two big liners arriving in the harbor. The harbor was dotted with boats of all sizes. That day was a profitable one for me, for with my boat I was carrying passengers in and around the places of excitement. There were two large battleship convoys which came with the liners on the days that they were landing the prisoners. The prisoners were escorted and taken off the liners in big brick barges from the lower harbor and brought up to the Navy Yard. The prisoners had large heavy navy blankets wrapped about them and just as fast as they went ashore they would throw them overboard. For a long time the blankets floated on top of the water, and then would disappear beneath it. Thousands of dollars in United

States taxes sunk to the bottom of the river with the blankets that the Navy had provided for the prisoners.

I recall the Spanish Admiral who stood out from all the rest. He was a little, sturdy fellow and very hard to handle. The guards had almost to carry him ashore the day of the landing. Yet, later, after he had been on the Island a short while, he was allowed to roam about on the mainland for short leaves.

People in masses were lined along the shore, eager to see what was going on. Everyone who could afford it, wanted to go out in boats so as to be close to the scene. Anyone was allowed to go on board the battleship for a specified two hours for inspection of the ship. Within this two-hour period, I had carried about one hundred people back and forth. There were a great many prisoners who were homesick, ill or mental brooders who died at the prison and were buried here. The Spanish authorities sent their own ships to carry the prisoners home after peace was declared. Here is a Portsmouth Navy Report of July 8, 1897, of the landing of Spanish prisoners:

"Col. Jos. Tarlig
reports temporary duty guarding prisoners of war.

At 2 P. M. of the 11th, 624 men and 2 surgeons, prisoners of war were landed on Seavey Ld. At 7 P. M. of the 12th, 7 Spanish officers were landed.

July 15th Harvard arrived at noon of the 16th. 910 prisoners were landed from her.

At noon of the 18th, 52 more prisoners were landed from her.

July 20th—16 Spanish men-of-war died since landing.

August 13—Rear Admiral Carvere of the Spanish Navy arrived leaving same day.

August 24—16 Spanish prisoners of war arrived.

August 25—Resolute arrived Battalion of Marines from Cuba landed next day."

(1898?)

"September 11:—Annapolis and liner 'City of Rome' arrived 1561 Spanish Ag. 12 prisoners of war embarked on City of Rome and sailed."

Thus perched upon its peninsula of industry and seafaring enterprise, Portsmouth has been one of the busiest places that has spread New England's fame. It housed the oldest newspaper of all the existing newpapers of the United States, the "New Hampshire Gazette," which started at Portsmouth in 1756, while the "Portsmouth Journal" was established in 1793. It has harbored a millenium of such instances of valuable epoch-making history. From the early Revolutionary Days to this new second World War, it has played its patriotic tune with a harmonious theme that has caused the many inshore Americans to dance to a safer and saner note of preparedness. Truly no City of the United States has placed its heart more into its line of duty and has accomplished so much of note throughout these centuries.

Portsmouth, to me, will always be my home town on the mainland. From the South End to the North End, from the wharf to the bridge, I wend my feet across its streets tending those thoughts of satisfaction that I was cast here to cast my lot.

CHAPTER III

"A heap of bare and splintery crags,
  Tumbled about by lightning and frost,
  With rifts, and chasms, and storm-bleached jags,
  That wait and growl for a ship to be lost.
  No islands; but rather the skeleton
  Of a wrecked and vengeance-smitten one."

—Lowell.

MY SEA of memory harbors its main ship forever at my home port on the Isles of Shoals. I woke up each morning of my early boyhood looking up at the bright, red, clear skies meeting the horizons of the ocean bed and blending with the rising sun the number of fishing dories which had before dawn dipped their way out into the hazy expanse of the waters and anchored. Life had no terrors for me when I went to sleep at night while watching the starting of lavender, red, and purple of the sun as it set below the horizon. Mirages of mists rose continually at twilight, enveloping the sky-lit prisms into cloaks of mystery while challenging on the night. As someone has written:

"White endless clouds of mist
  Over the lighthouse, floating drifts;
  Hugging all to its shadowy bosom,
  Sealing within a silvery blossom;
  When, pierced by the setting glint of the sun,
  Two golden masts are born,
  Silhouettes, reflecting spun
  By the Almighty One."

[11]

Sunshine or storm the Isles manifested its beauty of nature and impressed me with its vivid pictures. Generally, the weather on the Isles of Shoals is of low temperature. It differs ten to fifteen degrees from the mainland and it is so changeable and moist that no ice can be raised. There is hardly ever a thunderstorm on the Isles of Shoals because the river on the mainland splits them in two and they go both ways; one west and one east. My idea is that these Isles are the best spot on the Atlantic Coast for health and comfort; so refreshing is the breeze that rises out of the ocean and the sun's rays have a violet ray effect upon one's vitality that rejuvenates the human energy.

The Isles are absolutely just rocks planted bleakly by some of nature's craftmanship in the midst of a section of the ocean vaulted over by an everchanging sky and completely surrounded by the blue, green, temperamental waves which at times lapped the shores in listing submission and at others would dash thundering against the shores in revolutionary tumult. No one seems to know exactly why they had been placed there so, but Sweetser in his book, "Along The Shore," claims that the Islands: "show a resemblance to the bald peaks of a submerged valcano thrust upward out of the waters, the little harbor being its crater." Whether or not this is true, or whether at some time in the history of the earth formation there may have been some overland connection which might have been later submerged through some upheaval of the ocean bed, or perhaps by the famous ice sheet which crawled over the continent, it is just a conjecture or merely an opinion.

I couldn't possibly describe the Isles of Shoals in any better or more picturesque manner than Celia Thaxter in her book, "Among The Isles Of Shoals."

"Appledore, called for many years Hog Island from its rude resemblance to a hog's back rising from the water, when seen from out at sea, is the largest and most regular in shape. From afar, it looks smoothly rounded, like a gradually sloping elevation, the greatest height of which is only seventy-five feet above big-water mark. A little valley in which are situated the buildings belonging to the house of entertainment, which is the only habitation, divides its four hundred acres into two unequal portions. Next, almost within a stone's throw, is Haley's Island, or 'Smutty Nose,' so christened by passing sailors, with a grim sense of humor, from a long black point of rock stretching out to the southeast, upon which many a ship has laid her bones. This island is low and flat, and contains a greater depth of soil than the others. At low tide, Cedar and Malagar are both connected with it,—the latter permanently by a breakwater,—the whole comprising about a hundred acres. Star Island contains one hundred and fifty acres, and lies a quarter of a mile southwest of Smutty Nose. Toward its northern end are clustered the houses of the little village of Gosport, with a tiny church crowning the highest rock. Not quite a mile southwest from Star, White Island lifts a lighthouse for a warning. This is the most picturesque of the group, and forms with Seavey's Island, at low water, a double island, with an area of some twenty acres. Most westerly lies Londoner's, an irregular rock with a bit of beach upon which all the shells about the cluster seem to be thrown. Two miles northeast from Appledore, Duck Island thrusts out its lurking ledges on all sides beneath the water, one of them running half a mile to the northwest. This is the most dangerous of the Islands and, being the most remote, is the only one visited to any great degree by the shy sea-fowl that are nearly banished by civilization."

The origin of the names of Gosport and Isles of Shoals is an interesting story: Ralph May in his "Early Portsmouth History" claims that "the name Gosport, which later was given to the township on Star Island, probably comes from Gosport, England, a little village half a mile over the water from Portsmouth, England. It was at Gosport, England, that on August 18, 1642, one of the first battles was fought between the forces of Charles I and Parliament. Quoting from Dickens, 'The war broke out at Portsmouth.' 'Annals of Portsmouth, England,' by W. H. Saunders states that a Lord Wentworth was one of the leaders of the Royal forces in the town at the time of this attack." Then May also writes about the beginning of the name of the Isles of Shoals that: "A word about the origin of this name, 'Isles of Shoals.' They are supposed to have been so called, not because of the ragged reefs run out beneath the water in all directions, ready to wreck and destroy, but because of the 'shoaling,' or 'schooling' of fish about them, which, in the mackerel and herring seasons, is remarkable."

The history of the Isles of Shoals, its scattered founding, settling and growth and decline, dates back to the days of Captain John Smith. There are many tales written about the first settlement of the Isles of Shoals. They were sighted by Gosnold in 1602 and by Martin Pringle in 1603. The famous French monarch Henry of Narvarre granted to Pierre de Guarst, Sieur de Monts, a patent for the entire territory. They were later landed upon by the Samuel de Champlain who later discovered Lake Champlain. They were noted down and carefully recorded on the map by Captain John Smith and were at one time named after him, the Smith Isles. In 1619, Sir Ferdinand Gorges and John Mason sailed along the New England coast and made a report of the Islands to the King of England.

L. Whitney Elkins in his "Story of Maine" writes that: "William Pepperell of Plymouth, England, came early to New England in a fishing vessel and established a business of handling fish on the Isles of Shoals. Later he moved across to Kittery Point where he married the daughter of John Bragg, tavern keeper, shipbuilder and man of means. Pepperell possessed little education but was gifted with great natural ability and energy which enabled him to extend his fishing enterprises and to engage in trade and commerce. At Kittery a son, also named William Pepperell, was born. The boy was brought up to assist in his father's business, which came into his hands more and more as time went on. Eventually, the younger Pepperell built wharves and warehouses in which he stored his cargoes and imports. From his shipyards nearby he sent vessels to every port of the commercial world. It is said, and truly, we believe, that as many as one hundred sails at a time were seen anchored in the harbor. He set up saw-mills and acquired land until he could travel many miles to the northeast without setting foot off his own possessions. He was military commander (thought he knew little enough of military tactics), local magistrate, and a strong pillar of the Congregational Church. He had been a member of the General Court at Boston, and withal he was a popular as well as a powerful man."

In the same book Elkins writes: "Doubtlessly these islands, surrounded as indeed they were with the best of fishing grounds, were visited by summer fishermen from the time of the Popham Colony. It is certain that by 1630 extensive provisions for curing fish had been made, that considerable stores of supplies for trade were kept on hand, and that Spanish ships came hither to load with fish for cities of Spain. It is probable that permanent settlement was made about that time. When Benjamin Hall, the excommunicated minister, preached there in 1641 it is supposed that the members of thirty or forty families composed his congregation. In 1653, when the islanders had come under the rule of the Puritan colony, though with ill grace, a local court was granted them for the trials of petty cases. The fishermen prospered and seven years later we are certain that Star, Smuttynose, and Appledore could boast of forty-eight families, a church edifice, and a settled minister."

Parsons writes that as the Islands became a receiving house for the fish and furs from other localities for shipment to England for the reception of goods for bartering with the Indians, clothing, rum, gunpowder, and other necessities of pioneer life for distribution to the other settlements—"So valuable had the Islands become at the time that Mason and Gorges made their final division of territory in 1635, Mason taking New Hampshire and Gorges taking Maine, that neither cared to surrender his entire interest in them to the other, and the group was divided between them precisely on the line to the province of Maine and Mason annexing the southerly half to the province of New Hampshire. This accounts for the strange division of this cluster of barren rocks between two states, a matter which has puzzled a great many people to account for."

Parsons again states that: "After the dissolution of the Laconia Company and the separation of Mason and Gorges, the Shoals continued to prosper. Many persons settled there, many dwellings were built, and the resident population ran up to about six hundred souls; 'they had a meeting house on Hog Island, a court house on Haley's Island, and a seminary of such repute that even gentlemen from some of the towns on the sea-coast sent their sons here for literary instructions." (Williamson's "History of Maine"). "The meeting house is said to have been of brick; the dwellings of the more substantial residents were comfortable and of good size, the furniture as ample as then known in New England, an ordinary, or tavern, was kept on Smutty Nose, a bowling alley on Hog

Island, and ale houses abounded." (York County Records). "The estates of the leading men at the Islands were at this time among the largest in New England."

So, from facts of history records, the Islands were famous and well known even in their early days—a mecca of leading and learned men who built up and enriched these Isles in their days of prosperity. At that time all the Isles seemed to share in this popularity but according to Parsons in the year 1680 there was the big migration of the islanders from one part of the islands to another. There was no apparent reason for it; but he supposed that the reason that they had migrated from the "northerly islands to Star Island" was that "Star Island was considered by the Islanders as being more secure from Indian attacks than Hog and Smuttynose."

"Star Island so prospered by this migration that in 1715 by the act of the provincial assembly of New Hampshire it was created a town, by the name of Gosport; and in 1720, of every 1,000 pounds raised in the province by taxation 20 pounds was assessed upon Gosport, a proportion which was maintained with but slight variations for many years. In 1767 the number of residents of Gosport was 284, of whom four were slaves."

In his "History of Rye," Parsons mentions the following: "About 1870 a large summer hotel, the Oceanic, was built on Star Island by the late John R. Poor, who had acquired title of the entire island with the exception of one dwelling and holding of land owned by John B. Downs. Mr. Poor was desirous of buying that property, also, but Mr. Downs, who was born and had passed his life on the Island and had seen a family of his own grown up around him there, was much attached to his home, and being in comfortable circumstances, financially, he declined to sell. The Oceanic, two or three years after it was built, took fire one night in the spring during a violent southeast storm, and was entirely consumed, as were also a number of uninhabited houses; but owing to the direction of the wind the house of Mr. Downs, though nearer the hotel than any others, escaped with a severe scorching. The Oceanic was immediately rebuilt, larger than before, but not on the same site. Mr. Downs had his house repaired and continued to live in it until a short time before his death, which took place at North Hampton on the 23rd of April, 1888 in the 77th year of his age. He was the last of the old stock of 'Shoalers' to retain a homestead in the town of Gosport, and he held it until the town went out of existence. After his death, and some years after Mr. Poor's hotel and surroundings had passed to other ownership, his heirs transferred his Star Island property to the new owners of the Island."

This John B. Downs was my grandfather of whom I shall write more further on. He was one who shared in the political influence of the affairs of the town; but it is my Uncle Levi who had the most interesting experiences in the field of politics. The following is an account by Parsons of the last town meeting:

"The last town meeting of Gosport was held on the 14th of March, 1876. The principal business of the meeting was, as had for some years been the case, the election of a representative to the legislature. There was no money to raise for roads, because there were no roads on the island; nor for schools, or fire, or police department, or street lights, for a similar reason. With little to do, and very few voters to do it, a brief and orderly session might reasonably have been expected; but instead of this the meeting was disorderly and riotous in an extreme degree, the offenders being, it was alleged, a number of employees of the hotel who came down from Boston that morning by steamer to vote, and concerning whose right to vote at the Island there was the gravest doubt. So serious was the disturbance that the moderator, after vainly endeavoring to restore order, peremptorily declared the polls closed, thus ending what was not only the last but probably the most turbulent town meeting ever held at Gosport. The certificate of election was given to Levi W. Downs, a son of John B. Downs, who took his seat when the legislature assembled; but a legislative investigation into the affairs of the town was instituted, the report being that so few legal voters as the town possessed should not be allowed a representative in the legislature, and the abolition of Gosport as a town was decided upon. But the rocky islets which comprised the town's entire territory could not be abolished and as they had to have a place in some town the bill which abolished Gosport annexed them to Rye, and declared vacant the seat in the legislature that had been occupied by the ancient settlement's representative. Not a single voter accrued to Rye in consequence of this annexation, no person ever claiming the right to vote in this town on the grounds that they lived or ever had lived on Star Island."

Just a short while before I was born, in and about the middle of the eighties, the fame of the Isles of Shoals was at its peak. Authors, poets, artists and men of wealth traveled from far to display their talents in this wealth of pictorial natural resources for the universal mind and the cravings of intellectual curiosity. To the hotel of the Laighton's which had been built in 1847 by Thomas Laighton on Appledore and to the later built Oceanic hotel at Star came the celebrities of the times such as James Russell Lowell, Richard Henry Dana, famous for being the author of "Two Years Before The Mast," Harriet Beecher Stowe, the famous judge and politician, Charles Levi Woodbury, as well as John Greenleaf Whittier, the noted American poet of rustic New England life who after his frequent visits with Celia Thaxter corresponded with her for the rest of his life.   Many others of equal celebrity not only in the field of literature but also in the field of business and politics stayed at these hotels for their summer resort and then migrated to the vicinity of Boston throughout the long winters.   These hotels were in reality salons of intellect, veritable Isles of Culture in a rough setting—inhaling the beauty in such a degree that much was contributed to the advancement of American literature.

The Isles of Shoals was no idle place in those days.   Everything seemed to hum in harmony to make it so.   I can remember back some of these noted people would come and stay all summer with their two masted sailing yachts.   As I look at the Isles of Shoals today I find that everything has changed.

The largest Island is Hog, which was called that in my younger days and which is now called Appledore, where the home of Celia Thaxter was and the Leighton family who in those days owned the biggest hotel, the Appledore, which was burned down in later years.   There were four hundred families and twenty large cottages; now there is nothing more than the coast guard to take care of the coast for miles around.   Then comes Star Island, the first place I ever landed and which was then called the town of Gosport with three hundred people on it.   It was one of the biggest fishing places in New England; now all that is left is one hotel, the Oceanic, that is opened for two months of the year under the Corporation sponsored by the Unitarian Church officials for worship and education in religious matters.   The Downs' cottage which was rebuilt after the big fire still stands and the keeper of the Oceanic remains there the whole year around.

Smutty Nose Island is the next in size.   This was where the Haley family lived in the early days and kept a tavern and grocery store.   Later a man named Lem Caswell kept a fish farm where fifty men would come to fish and stay for the summer. In those days two large steamers ran from Portsmouth two trips a day; but now not one family lives there. Next came Langder which was for fifty years owned by the Newton family. This was a great fishing island; but not a soul is living there now. Cedar Island is the only island where at one time there were any trees growing on it. They have all died, but the stumps still remain standing. One family of the boys go lobstering, descendents of the Caswell and Newton families. White Island was where a red and white light used to flash in turning every three minutes and used to flash into my bedroom on the Island but a big bulb flashes from the lighthouse now. Years ago there was a family by the name of Robinson who went out lobster fishing from this Island but now all that remains there are the sea gulls roosting about.

In spite of all these changes, I would like to live on these Shoals all over again. The same old rocks are still my view although I have been within a mile of them about every day for thirty years. I have never frequently landed there although my business has brought me within hailing distance. I never land there, for it is not the same. Most of the old shoalers have all passed on. My brother and I are all there are left of those who knew those old times. I still think that I would like to go back and spend the rest of my life out there where everything is so peaceful and quiet. When I drive down to the beach and look out toward these Isles I yearn to be there. I meet people and talk to them and tell them that I was reared up on those islands, nine miles out to sea and am well proud of it.

CHAPTER IV.

WHISPERS WINDWARD

"The character and habits of the original settlers for industry, intelligence, and pure morals have acquired for them great respect in the estimation of posterity."—Williams' History of Maine

THE SHOALERS were always very cautious people who had the fear of the sea in their very bones and would not for the most part ever start upon any adventure which they knew was foolhardy. There was never a faint heart among them. My grandmother would often sit with a gun upon her knee, to be ready to shoot at anyone in time of trouble, for she had as good an aim as any man on the Isles. And my grandfather showed his courage and endurance when, on a stormy night, with the wind raving and the rain coming down in torrents, he heard frantic calls of distress from a shipwrecked vessel having foundered a short distance out from the rocks. He grabbed a rope and by some means managed to get the rope out to the ship to which it was fastened; and then he looked about to find a cornice of a rock or a projection of some sort to which to bind his end. It being along the smooth bleak crevices and the water washed rocks, he found none. He fastened the rope tightly about his waistline and wading waist deep out into the ravaging waters, with the rain pouring down over his southwester, with all his strength he held that rope fast until the shipwrecked men, one by one, had ferried themselves across. There could be no real fear among them, or in their hearts, for throughout their hardships these people fought and withstood any obstacle of man or nature with which they were confronted.

Morally, without police or law protection of any sort, with few rules of conduct and living in an isolated condition, the Islanders were very decent folk. In comparison they were far more upright and law abiding to the rules of convention than those at the same time in our cities, who under the tomahawk of protection and law, incessantly filled their jails to capacity. There were spats, there were quarrels, as in any community. There were the fools and the bright to be scoffed at and to be respected. There were the hale and the hearty, rugged, sun-burned, and there were the undersized, pindly, ill, who thrived as well as might be without constant medical care which in that century was even denied to the wealthy on the Mainland because of the lack of medicine and surgical skill. There were the free thinkers and the strictly religious. There were those who were popular among their neighbors and there were those who through some misdemeanor were taboo by the others. There were some who drank and some who would not touch a drop under the threat of death. There were the men who listened respectfully to the solicitous advice of the visiting missionaries, who frequently came over to save their souls from utter destruction, and men who inwardly withheld their own fixed ideas of what was right and what was wrong. There were racial differences of living of Swede, Finn, Norwegian, Scotch and English, all seafaring peoples who blended their customs into one solid whole. They were a crude people but a civilized and an original people, rugged and as stalwart as the sea surrounding them.

There were but very few idlers. For of all manners of work, fishing when it is carried on on a large scale as it was then, was a large enterprise and netted thousands of dollars in profits. All worked from early morning until late night. Men were ready at all times for any call of need. Women, realizing the number of hours that their men had to go out

on long fishing trips, helped them when they came in with a
load. It was they who worked alongside the men, slicing
and drying the fish, baiting hooks and making nets, just
as today the modern woman works alongside her husband
in the factory to help the household along. Each and every
family did their bit. If not in one way, they did it in another.
Sewed, baked, dug in together. Sometimes they would chaw
at one another, sometimes they refused to be on speaking
terms but always in time of need and work, they all hauled
in their bits together. A thriving sect as they weathered life.
True, some died of consumption, some of drowning, some
were lost at sea and never heard from, some even committed
suicide, and some more than the others lived to a ripe,
natural, old age.

There were courtships among them and there were marriages, many of which were performed by the famous Minister
Tucke whom they all loved and revered so well. I don't
remember, as I was too young, as to how the early Shoaler
courted his belle; but Celia Thaxter has written about a story
that was handed down to her.

"Very ancient tradition says that the method of courtship
at the Isles of Shoals was after this fashion: If a youth fell
in love with a maid, he lay in wait till she passed by, and
then pelted her with stones, after the manner of our friends
of Marblehead; so that if a fair Shoaler found herself the
centre of a volley of missiles, she might be sure that an ardent
admirer was expressing himself with decision certainly, if not
with tact! If she turned, and exhibited any curiosity as to
the point of the compass whence the bombardment proceeded,
her doubts were dispelled by another shower; but if she went
on her way in maiden meditation, then was her swain in
despair, and life, as is usual in such cases, became a burden
to him."

The Islanders married at an early age and very often married the girls from the Mainland whom they met in their trips to and from shore, so that inter-marriage between the Islanders was an exception rather than a rule.

Due to their ambitious and working temperaments food was always plentiful on the Isles. Their larders were always full. In summer it was customary to stock up the cellar for the oncoming long winter months. My grandmother's cellar was a cornucopia of food. Strings upon strings of dried apples would be hanging down. Hams upon hams would be cured and swaying there. Cakes of butter that my grandmother had churned, pickled herring and salted mackerel, dried cod fish by the stacks, barrels and barrels of flour and corn meal, sugar, lard and molasses, barrels of salt pork and bags upon bags of pea beans and potatoes, tea, coffee and everything else that was to be used for the winter except a large supply of beef. Beef was a luxury and for some reason or other was never to be had.

We youngsters as we were growing up always had our fill in eating. There was no fancy food, just plain ordinary, wholesome food and plenty of it. Corn meal was our mainstay. Hasty pudding and molasses were to be had at any time of the day. Milk was not plentiful as there was not enough vegetation on the Isles to feed amply more than one or two cows and these were not sufficient to provide the milk for the many people there. The long, cold-locked winters prevented the Shoalers from being able to sail after their milk and often the Island was without milk except for the wee children.

Black coffee was the standard drink. As in the cold countries of Europe, black coffee and coffee in any form is drunk to warm and stimulate the temperature of the body, so the fishermen coming in from the biting cold of the salt breezes drank their black coffee to warm up their in'ards. Of all the hundreds drinking black coffee on the Island there were very little ill effects as most of the men were well over six feet tall and weighed well over two hundred pounds.

The sharp winds had also made the hardy men and women adopt and pursue another custom which is usual in the homes of the Swedes and Norwegians of the old country. Under no pretext were the windows ever opened during the winter; cracks and crevices were caulked up so that the sweeping gales were kept outside. The long winters kept us enclosed without proper air and ventilation until the spring thawed us out. Yet, as with people in the Nordic countries, we survived and were none the worse, for coal and wood were scarce and the breezes strong and freezing.

During these long stays within doors we children were brought up among the sayings of the elders who, to admonish us and to impress us with the sums of their life's experiences throughout the years, would repeat them over and over. They had been told to them and we, in our turn, were to tell them to our children. If we should accidentally twist an empty chair around with our fingers, as we were apt to do so often, we would be sure to be reminded that for some unforeseen reason or other we were to receive a licking before the day was out, and if turning to the empty rocking-chair, we should rock it back and forth, then bad luck would visit our household.

Longing for company the Shoalers had many ways of predicting the coming of strangers. If a broom fell across the door, if my mother dropped a dishcloth on the floor, or if in the process of eating you should unconsciously drop your knife, fork, or spoon, a stranger would be coming. A knife would be a man, a fork would be a woman, and a spoon would be a child. Should a sharp instrument fall to the floor and stick in it, and pointed to certain directions then from that direction the stranger was to come whether North, South, East or West, from the Mainland, from Portland or from some distant port.

Singing at the wrong time was always a sign of something that was to happen. If you sang before breakfast you would cry before supper. If you sang while eating your meal at the table then bad luck was a certainty. No fisherman wanted you in his crew if before starting out on a trip, you were singing lustily before eating your breakfast.

Bad omens were about us on every turn. If you changed your customary place at the table, if you put up an umbrella inside the house, or if you failed to give a copper in return for the gift of a knife, you would be persecuted by thoughts of bad luck. Often, oh, so often, we children would become hilarious and boisterous in our play and our mother would always stop us with a sober tone of: "Stop, stop, you children, you are too happy, something is going to happen." And so our spirits were squelched, our minds quieted down into a feeling of awe and expectation of the dreadful.

Another well known superstition of the Isles was that when you had wound up a clock and after a short time it stopped, something was to happen. Good luck always came in the same mysterious way. If you stubbed your toe going upstairs, and if you saw a pin lying on the floor, you were supposed to repeat: "See a pin, pick it up, and all the day you'll have good luck."

Death was to be seen approaching from every angle. If a dog howled in the night it was a sure sign. And if a bird from the shoals would strike against the windowpane with all of its little might to get in, it was certain you would soon hear of a passing. If a portrait of a person were to fall without due cause, that person would have something happen to him or would pass away in a short time. To look out of a window and to think that you see someone coming in and there isn't anyone, the person whom you are supposed to see has passed away or is in danger. Knocking at the door and going to see who is there and to find no one is also a certain sign. My mother had an actual experience in the substantiating of this belief. While she was busy cooking a kettle of mince meat one morning at ten o'clock when she was living in Newburyport, Mass., she heard a knocking at the kitchen door. The knocking startled her; she went quickly to open the door and found no one there. Later that same morning news was brought to her that her brother, Frank Caswell, had died at ten o'clock in Portsmouth.

Many events centered about the keeping of the Sabbath Day. If the fishermen had not gone to worship at the regular service on Sunday then they were not expected to get a large haul of fish during the following week. Above all, not one of us ever dared to drive a nail on Sunday for that would bring on a shower of bad luck. Over in Eliott, Maine, many years ago my Aunt Julia Brooks, who had married one Leslie Brooks, and who was the sister of my Grandfather Caswell, would not lift her hand except from pure necessity on the Lord's Day. She would ceremoniously set the table on Saturday night, with piles of clean dishes in the center, and would not clear it off until the following Monday morning. Bible reading was her pastime and she refrained from wearing any finery at any time.

In spite of all these whims and fancies, good pure Yankee ingenuity prevailed over the Isles. I well remember the paper lighters my grandmother and grandfather used to have piled above their stove. They were small pieces of paper rolled up very, very tight. They would be used by the household for matches and it was quite a trick to roll them up into the right tightness and thickness.

These are some of the whispers floating from the windward side that breeze through my mind. Whispers of the times that were. Character and habit form so much of a lifetime, ambition and industry, diligence and negligence, whims and beliefs, help them while the climate carves us into what we become and our ideas are built up around them. So were the Shoalers, in such a way were they built up and thus my grandfather and my grandmother played their part in the cinema of the Isles.

CHAPTER V

MY GRANDPARENTS, bless their souls, centered about my whole early life. The last two years I spent on the Isles of Shoals were with them as they were the last to leave the Island, much against their will for to them the Isles were their life—they constituted the real old shoalers. Later on they were forced to resettle reluctantly in their newly bought home on the mainland at Portsmouth.

They lived their time on Star Island in the Downs' homestead which they, themselves, had had built. The homestead was built on the high land of Star overlooking the wharf and commanding full sight of the landing. It was a white, two-story cottage of large, square dimensions, there being four rooms up and four rooms down which at that time was considered, especially on the Isles, a large dwelling. There was a long, wide porch extending from one end of the front of the house to the other. There was a lane which ran from the house to the barn with large willows, the only trees that would grow on the island, bordering each side. The house is still standing at Star and is now known as the Downs' cottage and is owned at present by the Unitarian Society where the keeper of the hotel lives the whole year round.

My grandfather came from the good old stubborn Yankee stock which has never fully forgotten its English accent. His name was John Bragg Downs. The Downs family dates back to an Edward Downs of Rye, New Hampshire. In an early "History of Rye" by Langdon Parsons, there is mention of a Downs in the following account: "It has always been said

Master Richard Locke, when out fishing on what was known as half-way ledge, saw a man on horseback come to James Goss'. He said the horse was white and told who the man was. It proved to be right. He was a man from up the country. It is also said one Downs could see the windows in a house at the Shoals from Sandy Beach, and told how many panes of glass there were in it. Old Master Locke also saw a boat coming around York Nubble, and told what boat it was and who were in it. It was some of our people who had been down East (Pemaquid) fishing. They must have been very peculiar days to see so far."

Edward Downs had four children, one of them being a Henry who married Abigail Bragg. She was born October 17, 1793 and lived at Gosport. Among their children was born John Bragg Downs in 1809 who married in 1834, Martha Olive Foss, my grandmother.

My Grandfather Downs was a man of medium size and weighed about 170 pounds. He wore chin whiskers and shaved on the side of his face. He never had a gray hair on his head even to old age. Naturally he was temperamental but in his later years he lost most of this and became much more taciturn and quiet. Although somewhat distant in many of his mannerisms he was very sociable and congenial, fond of fun and full of life. He was a leader among the men of Star Island and whenever they wished to know anything or needed help of any kind they went to consult him and he was always sure to find some out for them. He had one characteristic which I shall never forget;—he drank a cup full of rum three times a day.

He was always a busy man. He was the manager of the fishermen who lived in the shanties on the Island. At that time he hired some thirty fishing men and he, himself, did not actually go out fishing very much. These men would go out fishing the year around and then, upon returning with their catch, would salt the fish and dry them on the Island. After the fish were dried and cured; they would put them in barrels and have large vessels come to get them to take the fish to the West Indies. In the West Indies the fish were traded for rum and molasses. The fishermen would not get their money until the rum and molasses were sold. So they would bring the rum and molasses to Portsmouth to sell. Then the fishermen would be paid for their amount of work at the end of the season.

My grandfather's main sport was to play chess, and for hours on end he would invite his friends in to play with him during the long winter months. He was a sturdy, strong man. When I was fourteen I did the work around and chopped the wood for him. It was all driftwood that I had gathered. In the Spring logs would come drifting up to the island—great big, huge logs. He and I would go and get them. We would put off in a boat and bring them in to chop them up. Sometimes they would be so large and compact my grandfather would blow them up with gunpowder.

He lived to the good ripe age of eighty. The last twenty-five years of his life he suffered from the common consumption of that time, for which he had been advised to take the doses of rum. During his life he had accumulated well over fifty thousand dollars. This amount of money at hand constituted a good sized fortune in the early nineteenth century when most bargaining was done by bartering of unnecessary goods, and he had invested in ample railroad stocks in the new Boston and Maine railroad. He kept his ready money in notes in a tin box on the Isles of Shoals.

He bought and had built two large sailing vessels, of which he was the sole owner. They were the two finest fishing vessels afloat in those times because they were the most modern in 1858. They were built on the Damiescottie River in the lower part of Maine by the Hodgon Mills. The "Albert Woodbury" was built in 1850, a large two master, and weighed thirty-two tons, costing forty-eight hundred dollars and which manned a crew of twelve to fourteen men. The "Agnes E. Downs" weighed eighty-two tons and cost eighty-seven hundred dollars and when equipped for fishing the entire cost of this vessel was one hundred thousand dollars. This vessel manned a crew of from sixteen to twenty men according to the kind of fishing. My grandfather also owned the controlling interest in the "White Rover" which was another large master fishing vessel. He owned an interest in the "Mary E. Caswell" which was commanded by Levi Downs and was lost on the rocks in Wells Bay, but all hands were saved. He had an interest in the sloop "Helena," which was owned by John Oliver Downs and commanded by Ephraim H. Downs, my father, as well as owning several small boats and all types of fishing gear—nets, trawls, seines, and hooks.

The investments of a fishing man in business in those times before the arrival of the steam engine and until the steam power was in wide use in ocean trading were of good standing. It is with the arrival and use of steam power that the investments of fishing were precarious and uncertain, for now it is easier to reach Boston and New York without having to stop at the lesser ports of New England as stopping off places or relay posts. My grandfather had quite a business of selling and renting vessels and crews for fishing and trading purposes, for as any fishing man grows more accustomed to the ways and means of fishing, others came for advice and would want to buy or hire a vessel from him to run and master with a crew of men. Sometimes, these vessels would stock from five to seven thousands of dollars in trips, at other times, they would not get fish enough to pay for their bills, but as it averaged up through the course of the years, they made a fairly good living.

Throughout my grandfather's life, my grandmother was forever his sturdy companion in whatever way it was possible. He managed the thirty fishermen but it was she who saw that they were fed regularly, for they lived in the fishing shanties along the edges of the Island. She did the main cooking for all of them and would care for them in times of sickness. She was at all times ready to administer to the sick and the needy on the Isles. Very often the story has been told me where, even though some of the women on the Island would not be on speaking terms with her, yet she would act as their midwife and not speak to them or speak ill of them. She had a spinning wheel upon which she spun all of her cloth and with which she tailored the men's trousers. She spun all of her own cloth and did all of her own sewing by hand and at the age of eighty she was just as smart with her sewing as in her young days.

She was a large sized woman weighing about two hundred and twenty-five pounds, which did not prevent her from being active and getting around. She was very energetic and quick and enjoyed seemingly very good health for I never heard of her having been ill. She always did her own housework in her very own ways and was very set in whatever she did do. She had one chair which she prized and no one else would be allowed to sit upon it. It was right next to the window from where she could see the steamers coming in from the Mainland. She would say: "Here comes the 'Appledore'!"

When the steamer would come by the point over towards the Island the pilot would blow the steamer's whistle to let them know how many passengers they were going to have for dinner. One long whistle meant ten persons and one short one meant five or so. So that when the steamer landed, the hotel managers knew just how many they had to seat and serve at the table as well as to provide adequate reservations. The steamer made two round trips a day. She would leave the Island at nine in the morning and return at noon and at three in the afternoon she would go to the mainland and return at six at night and tie up at the wharf for the night. There was an orchestra continually playing with dancing going on with all sorts of games being played. Then the Isles were a gay affair with about three hundred guests coming and going in the Hotel at all times. When the steamers would land, the wharf would be crowded with guests. People of all walks of life were coming and going all the time. There was everything about to make one happy. There were plenty of sailing vessels and boats of all kinds to make the scenery colorful and entertaining. That is why my grandmother so carefully reserved her chair by the window.

Before her marriage her name was Martha Olive Foss. Her direct ancestors came from Rye also. The first Foss in Rye of which Langdon Parsons writes was a John Foss who: "was said to have arrived at Boston in a British war vessel from which he jumped overboard and swimming ashore, ran away. He thought of settling at a place called Reid's Temple but not being pleased with the location, came to Rye, where he was admitted into the family of John Berry, and married his daughter. It is said that twelve children were born to them, one son settling in Maine, near Scarborough, where he was drowned. A John Foss was at Dover in 1665, served on the grand jury in 1688, and died in 1699."

Then there is the story of Job Foss, grandson of John Foss, who married in 1750, a Sarah Lang. It seems that once on a special time he let "a tame Indian stay in his house one night and the board to which the Indian was tied caught on fire and came near burning a child and a house." My grandmother

was a direct descendant of these Fosses. Her father was Job
Foss born in 1785, and who married a Patty Berry, who lived
also at Rye in, I believe, the vicinity of Sandy Beach.

She had three sons whom she worshipped, Ephraim Henry,
Oliver and Levi. Each of these boys had a bedroom and
when they were away she would shut each individual bedroom
up and until they returned she allowed no one to disturb them
or even to enter them. She also had two daughters, Eliza and
Sarah. My grandmother had her heart all set on Sarah marry-
ing the minister, but just before the wedding day she went
off and married one Charles Hidden. This same Sarah was
the mother of young Charles Hidden who served as pastor of
the Carver Baptist Church for many years in Middleboro,
Massachusetts. He graduated from the Vermont Medical
College and became a practicing physician in Newburyport,
Massachusetts. He afterwards became an evangelist and
studied for the ministry, being ordained as a Baptist minister.
He also was the head of a newspaper syndicate and was the
author of several books.

In 1925, he dedicated a section of cranberry bog at Carver
to be known as "God's Cranberry Bog," the proceeds of which
were to be used in the study of religious work. He died at
the age of seventy-nine at his home on Everett Street in
Middleboro.

My cousin, Agnes Downs Flaherty, daughter of my Uncle
Levi, wrote me an incident that she remembered about the old
homestead and my grandmother. She wrote me as follows:
"The fire happened when my brother Albert was two years
old. He was one of the children that had to go out in the
terrible winter weather. Aunt Eliza and her two children
also were there. Mother said that the night of the fire, grandmother got up to tend one of the children and saw the blaze.
They only had time to get out in anything they could find.

They wrapped the children in bedclothes and a featherbed which caught fire as they got out the back door. They pushed the featherbed in the big rain barrel at the door. They had to go to the highest point to escape the flames, so fierce was the wind blowing the flames of the hotel toward them. They later took refuge in the parsonage (which they broke into) until help came in from Portsmouth. There they found the hotel's crockery and linen stored up. So they got permission later to help themselves to what they needed. They also lost about two hundred dollars worth of sewing materials, such as cloth for dresses, sheets, pillow slips, towels, etc., and all the products which they always stored up for the winter."

I have one chair from the old Star Island school, also have two ladderback chairs, old standing stool and family cradle that belonged to grandmother's family. These things were in the kitchen when the old house burned; and were the only things saved. You know the house that was lived in by Mose Laighton was the Downs' home.

Father said that there were one hundred or more people living on the Island when he was a boy. He used to tell how, when church services were going on, someone would go to the church and say that a school of fish had been seen, all the men would get up and leave, no matter if the minister were preaching.

My grandparents were a grand old couple. They lived a good, long, honorable life together and were the last to leave the Island to settle in a newly bought home in Portsmouth. They both dreaded to leave but as their age demanded care and could not withstand the hardships and loneliness, they had to leave with heavy hearts. They did not live long after their departure and at the time of my grandmother's death the following article was written in the "Daily Evening Times" in 1890.

"The Daily Evening Times, Saturday Evening, February 22, 1890, Published at Portsmouth, N. H.

OLD GOSPORT

DEATH OF MARTHA O. DOWNS

BRINGS UP SOME VERY INTERESTING REMINISCENCES
THE WRECK OF A RUSSIAN BRIG OFF
WHITE ISLAND LIGHT

"The death in this city, on the 17th inst., of Mrs. Martha O. Downs, at the ripe age of 80 years and 7 months, has already been noted in the 'Times;' and it has been stated that she and her husband, the late John Bragg Downs, were among the last of the old-time Isles of Shoals people to retain and occupy a homestead on the Islands. They were the very last; and the death of Mrs. Downs seems to be the snapping of the last thread which connected the ancient and once quite important, but now extinct town of Gosport, with the present time. When the late John R. Poor bought up all the rest of Star Island, preparatory to erecting the first Oceanic Hotel, Mr. Downs and wife declined to part with the homestead where they had passed so many happy years; where their children had been born and reared; and whence they had gone out to make homes for themselves elsewhere; and where they hoped to end their days. One terrible stormy night their dwelling was destroyed by the great fire which started in the hotel and swept that and a number of other buildings away, and would have consumed most of those that escaped had not the howling southeast gale which prevailed when the fire commenced, changed suddenly into an equally furious northwester. The remainder of that winter the elderly couple were compelled to pass with one of their sons in this city, but before another winter arrived they were back again in a reconstructed home on the rugged island they loved so well. With this exception, they never passed a winter on shore, though long and earnestly urged by their children to do so, until some four or five years ago when the increasing physical infirmities of great age made it impossible for them longer to remain at the island during the inclement season and they reluctantly yielded to the persuasions of their friends and 'came in, just for the winter.' A year or so ago the old gentleman died and from the time she who had been the sharer of his joys and sorrows faded rapidly away until rest came. Almost the last connected sentence which she spoke, not many hours before the end, showed that the enfeebled and wandering mind had carried her back to the days of her early womanhood, when with loyal, wifely love she had watched for the coming home of her life's partner.

"Mr. Downs was the hero of a story familiar to all of the old Shoalers, one which some years ago appeared in print in a newspaper of another city; as it has never been published here, its recital as it was related to the writer by Mr. Downs himself between fifteen and twenty years ago, will interest at least one class of the 'Time's' numerous readers. One night in March, at the time a Mr. Haley was keeper of White Island lighthouse, Mr. Downs was running the light for the keeper, who had 'gone to America' (as the Shoalsmen used to call the mainland) to get his family. There was only one keeper to a lighthouse at that time, lenses and machine lamps not having been invented at that time, and no watch was kept; the lamps were got to burning allright, the revolving gear was wound up if the light was a revolving one, and the keeper then went to bed, first setting an alarm clock to rouse him at the hour set for him to visit and trim his lamps, of which there were sometimes from fifteen to twenty. Mr. Downs had with him that night on the island, for companionship, another Shoalsman, and they sat up in the house until a late hour of the night, talking and listening to the screeching of a violent south-easter, the thunder of the waves as they dashed against the island, and often over a large part of it, and the pattering of the heavy snowflakes and particles of frozen spray against the wooden outside shutters of the front windows. As the companion was getting ready to go to bed he remarked to Mr. Downs, 'Well, John, what would you think if somebody was to knock at the door just now?' No one who knows what such a storm as was then raging really means on that wretched rock, can wonder that Mr. Downs answered, 'Think! I should think it must be the devil himself, for no human being could land on White Island this night and live.'

"At this instant was heard a rapping at the door—a loud, unmistakably urgent rap, and the sound was one that cannot be imitated, that made by human knuckles coming in contact with wood. The startled islanders sprung to their feet and looked at each other a moment, when the rapping was repeated, even more vigorously than at first, and with the remark that 'this is no kind of a night to keep even the devil outdoors,' Mr. Downs picked up the lantern and went to the door, not, he confessed, without serious misgivings as to what he might see when he got the door open. What he did see was not particularly reassuring. The old whale-oil lantern only served to make the darkness a little darker, but he could see two glittering eyes and beneath them a set of gleaming white teeth; but in an instant came a voice—a real, human voice: 'Brig ashore right here, sah!' The stranger was a gigantic negro nearly naked, and being taken into the house soon told his story. A Russian brig, loaded with hides and tallow, bound for Salem, had struck on the southwest point of the island in the snowstorm, while she was supposed to be a hundred miles from land. For a time after she struck the crew could only see a small rock under the bow, over which

the waves often made a clean sweep; then as the snow lightened a little, they saw the lighthouse, seemingly almost over
their heads. As the only hope of making their peril known,
the negro had let himself down from the bowsprit end with a
rope, and when he saw from the blackness beneath him that
the sea had gone out, he slid quickly to the rock and scrambled
in the darkness to find a higher point before the next sea
should come in, in which he was happily successful, and from
his new position discerned the light shining through the un-
shuttered end window of the dwelling, and proceeded cau-
tiously toward it. How he ever reached the house, over such
a route and on such a night, Mr. Downs could never fully
understand; but reach it he did.

"The negro was hastily clothed, and the three men, with
lanterns, were soon on the point near the brig; a line thrown
ashore was caught and held by the three, there was nothing to
make it fast to, not even to take a turn around, and down it
the rest of the brig's crew, which numbered fourteen persons,
all told, slid to rock and safety. When daylight broke the
brig had utterly disappeared, not so much as a chip of her
being left on the island. She had probably been lifted off the
rocks by a heavy sea on the rising tide—fortunately for her
crew it was ebb tide when she struck—and sank in deep water
before going very far. Broken spars, casks of tallow, hides
and other wreckage, were found scattered along the beach
from Hampton to the Merrimac River, for weeks afterward,
and no doubt came from the wrecked brig. It was more than
a week after the wreck before the weather was such that a
boat could leave or land at the island, and Mr. Downs said he
began to fear, along toward the last, that all hands would
starve. Mr. Haley's trip in was partly to renew his stock of
provisions, which was running rather low before he went;
and the stock which was small for one man had very little

show in the presence of sixteen. But fortunately they were able to get aid before they were very hard pushed, though Mr. Haley on his return found in his larder nothing he would have to carry over to another season."

CHAPTER VI

MY FATHER AND MOTHER

MY FATHER and mother were lovers, as well as their fathers and mothers before them, of that irresistible charm and freedom of the Isles of Shoals. There was nothing that felt so refreshing to the ruddy cheeks of my father as that salt wind blowing up out of the ocean; and, next to the odor of her mince meat, my mother liked nothing better than that salt twang that floated through the air. To him straddling about the rocks and talking politics was his idea of paradise, and to her attending the little church with a newly made bonnet with a brightly colored rose or ribbon was her seventh heaven. Both sensed that understanding of happiness on the island.

My father was a large built man with a continuous ruddy complexion and was about six feet tall and weighed well over two hundred and ten pounds. He had a round, jovial face and wore the traditional goatee of that period. Despite his size he was an extremely active man and died with his boots on. He was a temperate man who neither smoke nor drank. He was set in all his ways and when the doctors informed him that he would have to drink whiskey to speed up his heart beat, as he had chronic trouble, he stubbornly refused to do so even in the face of threatening death. He lived for providing his family; being very good and very kind and too kind, if anything. He would help to do wherever it was needed; even to emptying his pockets at the time. There is a story that I remember being told to me that there was a relative on the Island who was in dire need but was far too proud to let anyone know or to accept any financial aid. My father, having heard of the circumstances from a stranger, went there for dinner. After he had left, the relative found a five dollar bill beneath the plate. This is just one typical instance of the generosity of my father.

He was born on the Isles of Shoals on Star Island, which at his time was named the town of Gosport. He lived all of his young life there among some three hundred people and sixty voters. When he was nine years old he was given a Bible because he was able to read it through. Throughout his life he prized this Bible, and it always meant a great deal to him for he was a man who sponsored educational learning in every form. Although he secured the main part of his education in the little schoolhouse and church, as well as from visiting school-teachers and tutors, he maintained that invisible yearning for knowledge.

At twenty-five years of age he was master of the fishing vessel the "Mary E. Caswell," with which they did the main trading back and forth from the mainland. This vessel was named for his mother-in-law, and was financed by the Caswell family. In 1871 at the age of twenty-five the degree of Master Mason was conferred upon him by the Free Mason Lodge. Later on, he became the captain of the "Albert Woodbury," the ship in which he led such a busy career as a fisherman and blustering captain. At one period he was branch pilot, appointed by the State of New Hampshire, to lead the big square-rigged ships in and out of Portsmouth Harbor. He would put out at night and lay out for them for some days. This was in the days of the big square-rigged ships. They had to be guided up through the river into Portsmouth from the ocean. Portsmouth is two miles in from the ocean on the Piscataqua River, that is noted for its great depth of water and never rises or lowers in the winter. It has approximately the depth of sixty feet. It is a landlocked harbor with a wide entrance and easy to get into with plenty of room. In my days I have seen from six to seven of these square-rigged ships lying at anchor there.

As a fishing man my father had many interesting experiences. He told me once of the time in the winter of 1860, a man by the name of John Hontvet and brother left the Island for the fishing grounds and that the weather was icy cold and a heavy wind was beginning to blow. Hours passed after the time they were due to return and the Islanders began to fear for their safety with the rising storm. They believed that they were unable to get back and had drifted off to sea. My father and the other men on the island became more than anxious for they realized that they would be lost forever and the only chance was to take the big vessel and go after them. By the time they were prepared to start off the wind was fast blowing up into a terrific gale. My father was the master and three other men launched out in the "White Rover," one of the large masted vessels. The waves were mounting steadily with every hour. With every moment passing meant fewer possibilities of even the "White Rover" being able to return. Finally, by nothing short of a miracle, they caught sight of the two men and with the boats zigzagging about them they picked them up in the midst of the raging sea. The weather was then so bad that they could not turn back so the only thing left to do was to let the vessel take her own course. So they all drifted on for hours at end. It was blowing so thick a snowstorm that none could see where he was going. But she was a good vessel and held her own in the deep with the crew wondering whether at some unforeseen moment she would strike the rocks and go under with all on board. After seemingly an eternity of drifting as the storm abated they finally landed on a sand bank having no idea as to their whereabouts. All struggled to shore and managed to reach there safely. They had a very difficult time in keeping the vessel afloat as it was ice covered and the water was still quite rough. Half-frozen they climbed up the sand hill to reach the top to see if they could see anyone or anything. My father said that when he did reach the top he was so weak that he rolled right down the other side. He was half-frozen then and that helped to save his life from the fall. Most of the men had some part of them frozen but they, as the weather cleared, reached shelter and returned home safely. To my father this was the closest shave of his life and he never forgot it.

Our fresh meat was generally the sea-fowl that flew over our heads. My father was a great gunner. Whenever my mother wanted fresh meat she would call to him, "Hen, get me some ducks." He would go to the next island and bring back dozens of large ducks. He was a great shot—he once killed thirty-eight ducks in number. We called them ducks and drakes and when dressed they would weigh about three pounds and were very tasty eating. My mother would fill our pillows with the feathers and also they would fill our feather beds. To the thrifty Islander these birds were profitable and useful.

Being cooked by my mother was one of the reasons that they proved to be so tasty. She was also a native of Star Island, her maiden name being Mary B. Caswell and she, too, spent her life there. Her father and mother managed the first hotel, the old Gosport House, which was later bought by William H. Poor and afterward burned down. During the same fire we had to leave our home and rebuilt it the same year. My Grandmother and Grandfather Caswell were grand old people, being of that extremely proud and unemotional type of English. They had a daughter, Julia, who was at that time considered to be the prettiest girl on the Isles of Shoals. She was as good and chaste as could be, possessing a loving personality and bewitching all those whom she met. However, she passed away early in life, having been unduly deceived by one with whom she was deeply in love, and died of a broken heart.

Mother went to the school on the Island and was reared in the Advent religion. The Reverend, pastor and teacher at that time, was the Reverend Peabody whom she admired for his never-ending work on the Island. She, also, in later life became a Baptist Advent in Portsmouth. She had a habit of wearing white gloves to church and when she reached there, she disliked to kneel down but she always said that one good thing about going to church was that everyone was the same there.

She was a small built woman, naturally short, and if I do write it, a very pretty woman. She had a passion for wearing small hats in preference to large wide ones. She, as my father, was of a very kind, congenial nature and she continually loved to sit and knit gloves and stockings for us youngsters. No tramp ever went past our home in Portsmouth. Some claimed that the first tramp coming through with the Spring had a way of marking the house so that the tramps following would know that something to be eaten could be secured there. No matter who he was, or what he looked like, if he came to the door and was hungry she would take him in and feed him a good meal.

At the age of eighteen she married my father and from then on reared nine children, six boys and three girls. They had a hard road but a happy one. One morning father went out early to go fishing. He strutted out of the house merrily, singing lustily, "Throw Out The Life Line." Several hours later my mother was preparing my brother-in-law's and my breakfast and was frying some flapjacks. Suddenly, as if intuitively, she turned to my brother-in-law and said anxiously, "Orrin, I wonder where Hen is. He should be in from fishing by this time."

My brother-in-law got up from his breakfast and went down to the wharf. There he found my father in his sloop, "Helena," lying prone, dead, having collapsed with a heart attack. It was on a cold, blustering day in November in 1898, and I, upon hearing that he was in the boat, rushed out without hat or coat, and ran without stop to the boat. My mother missed him in every manner and life was never the same to her afterwards. Yet, she died at the age of eighty years, and did not rejoin her husband until she lay beside him in the old South Cemetery in Portsmouth. On the tombstone of my father is the following:

Capt. Ephraim H. Downs
died
Nov. 12, 1898
Aet. 58 yrs. 10 mos.

"They steered their course to the same good shore,
Nor parted long and ne'er to part no more."

In this picture is my dog, Taran, a german collie, who went with me when I would go to get a basket of lobsters. He would help me by taking hold of the handle and when I came in from fishing, he would come and bring me my coat. The man about my own age who is standing in the door is the one who helped me build my boat, there is also my grandchild, Victor and my daughter, Pearl.

This lobster house is about one hundred years old. You can see the lobster bait barrels. For years this has been the landing place for lobsters. It is close to the water. The barrels are full of fish for lobster bait of all kinds. There is a certain kind of fish with more oil that the lobster prefers.

CHAPTER VII

MY CHILDHOOD

MANY MAY think that the life of a boy on an island with only a few hundred people must have been a very lonely one. Mine was not such. Although there were very few children with whom to play, I found pleasure in watching the changes of nature and in doing my daily round of work among the fishing folk. Having arrived at the Island at the age of twelve days, I remained there until I was about fourteen, when we moved in to the mainland.

As other children, I had my ups and downs and my bumps. On Star Island there were two large reservoirs which caught the rain water in the rainy season of the year to supply the hotel with its water. One of these reservoirs was right in back of my aunt's house and one day, while walking too near the edge, I fell into the reservoir, which was deep with very smooth walls. There was no way for me to get out so I yelled and yelled as loudly as I could. My aunt happened to hear my frantic yells and she came with a pole for me to hold onto until she could get the men to come and pull me out. She went, the men came and laughingly fished me out; I was no worse for the wetting but a little more careful the next time.

Another time when I was about nine years of age I was playing on the wharf at Star Island. As to how I fell off, I can't remember, but I did fall into nineteen feet of water below, where there was solid rock. Some one saw me fall, and rushing over he pulled me out, unconscious. For a while, they gave me up. Excited and arguing in no uncertain tones, the fishermen worked over me, urgently pumping, until I came to. That was my first real taste of the deep.

From that time on I grew up with the fishermen who came in and went out of Gosport Harbor. There were about thirty fishermen on the Island. They would come from Hampton and Seabrook to catch fish to salt. In the Fall they would go home to the mainland for the winter. I would help them bait the trawls for the next day's fishing trip. They would bring back the small fish to me for helping them. I would take the sounds off them, clean and dry them, and when we went in to the mainland I sold them to buyers who bought them to make glue.

At about the age of eleven we moved to Smutty Nose island. My oldest brother had gone off in a fishing vessel. I would help my other brother in his work. Sometimes we would have a great deal and other times we would not have so much.

We lived in the same house where the Wagner murder was committed. I was a child of three years old and living at Star when the murder, which has become so famous as a treat murder story, was carried out on Smutty Nose Island on the night of March 5, 1873. Naturally, I have no recollection of the happening but from what I have heard and read since concerning it. John Hontvet and his wife, Maren, with her sister, Karen Christensen, and his brother, Matthew, and also Karen's brother, Ivan, living with his young bride, Anethe, were living with him on Smutty Nose. There was no one but them living there at the time on the island and the dark murky fog in the mysteries of the night enveloped this Island with a feeling of awe and sinister adventure.

John Hontvet never left the women alone on the Island unless it was absolutely necessary for him to do so, but in fishing it was often necessary for him to remain on the mainland because of the weather and distance. Previously to a few months before, to offset this and to offer more subsistence for his family, he had been boarding a Louis Wagner, a Prussian, who because of his similarity in race to the Norwegians, had been welcomed into their home as a friend and helpmate, and often he had proved to be of aid and protection as he was a tall, burly, steel-blue eyed Prussian of brute force with a clear calculating mentality. He had been in America for only about seven years and about his past life, nothing was known. He made his living by working in and about the shores, loading and unloading goods, and by fishing or hiring himself out as a crew member. At this particular time he had been out of work for some time and was in desperate need of money, having left the Hontvets just shortly before to board in Portsmouth on Water Street. So that it was no wonder then, when the men about the water front with whom Wagner spoke that night, heard him talking about his lack of money and his willingness to commit murder to get hold of some, they shrugged their shoulders and paid no attention to what seemed to them to be idle boasting.

John Hontvet had to carry in a haul of fish to Portsmouth late that afternoon which they had just caught on a trip and they, the three men, had to remain in Portsmouth waiting for the bait train to come in from Boston. The train was quite a bit later than usual so when Louis Wagner met them at the wharf in Portsmouth as they were waiting, they told him of their intention of having to stay in that night. Little did the three men dream of what was to happen to them when they did return home when they uttered these few innocent words which meant so much to the evil heart of the man beside them.

Banks were not relied in because they seemed so far away on the mainland, and most of the Shoalers hoarded and banked their money as best they could—in tin boxes, between mattresses, feather beds or sheets or otherwise. As a general rule most folk out there were hard-faring honest people and would loathe to touch the cent of another so that robbery on the Island was an unheard of crime. The Hontvets and family hid their money that they had brought over from Norway in much the same manner, leaving some out for daily use and placing the large sum of fishing money for each trip away in a trunk between two sheets. Wagner knew that they had money hidden there although he did not know the exact spot where it was hidden so this in the main, in his poverty-stricken, unemployed, bewildered mind he was forced to go to the extent of stealing a dory from the wharf and begin rowing with his powerful strong arms toward the silent island where the sisters were sleeping.

This was about half-past seven in the evening when he slid, with the raving ideas of a demon sweeping his mind, to the off shore of Smutty Nose and under cover of the darkness of the night he slipped onto the shore and made his way towards the blackened house. Maren, Anethe, and Karen, had retired at that time, not having any fear of being alone and being partially guarded by their small dog Ringe. There was a white blanket of snow still left on the Island from the winter's storms lending a softened still about them. Karen was sleeping in the kitchen while Maren and Anethe were sleeping in the room next to it. Suddenly, out of the stillness rose the piercing yelps of the dog ringing through the crisp air with a startling vibration. Karen was the first to hear him and she jumped up out of her bed. At first upon hearing the dog she thought that it was just her husband returning from the mainland so she called out into the pitch blackness: "John, John, is that you?"

With her cry Maren and Anethe awakened, and they became startled into terror when they heard the tearing fall of a chair being hurled at Karen, and the sound of a heavy form of a man dashing at full speed toward her. They heard the clock being struck from the shelf "a clock found later to have stopped at seven minutes after one."

Again they heard blow after blow and Karen cried out: "John kills me! John kills me!" for in the pitch blackness of the night she could think only that her husband was there.

Maren and Anethe rushed out of their bed to find that the door of their room had been in some way wedged. While they were trying to force it open they heard the horrible cries of Karen as she staggered across the floor and went down and loosened the bar that held the door.

As Maren went through the door she tried to seize her sister to drag her into the bedroom but the man looming over them with his huge shape and a chair still swinging high in his hand, uttered no sounds but kept on striking at them.

She dragged her sister into the other room and slammed tight the door. Meanwhile, Anethe climbed out of the window to cry for help from God knows where as the other Islanders were far away and fast asleep. She was in her nightgown and bare feet. She tried to yell, but fear paralyzed her throat so that she could not utter a sound. Wagner had seen her leave and he raced out of the house toward her. Upon seeing his full form silhouetted with the dim lighting afforded her by the snow, she found her voice to cry out:

"Louis! Louis! LOUIS!"

Upon realizing that he was recognized, he switched back into the kitchen and seizing an axe with which they had been chopping ice from the well that day, he ran back to the terror-stricken girl and cleaved her skull in two with all of his massive moronic strength wielding the axe.

Maren saw all this from the window and she tried to rouse Karen, who was by this time fully unconscious from fear and the blow she had received. Finding this to be impossible Maren took a blanket about her shoulders and hugging to her bosom the dog who was crouching beside her, she climbed out the bedroom window and stumbled half blindly through the snow to hide among the crevices of the stones in a cove near the edge of the island. As she was settling down to hide, she could hear the pitiful cries of Karen who was being carefully and artfully disposed of by the blood-thirsty German.

Wagner tracked about the house, looking this way and that for the missing girl. Being unable to find her, he returned to the cottage and, in the presence of the two bleeding bodies, he calmly brewed a cup of tea and ate some lunch that he had brought with him. After satisfying his appetite, child-like, he ransacked the rooms for the money and found less than twenty dollars to pay him for his trouble. Pocketing this with a grunt of dissatisfaction he coolly returned to his dory and rowed back to Portsmouth during the blackness of the early morning.

Maren, still hugging the dog close to her, waited until the sun was up before she tried to secure help. Upon hearing the pounding of the hammers of the workmen who were rebuilding the "Oceanic" after the great fire, she rushed to the edge of the island toward them and frantically called for help, while waving her blanket at them to attract their attention, but they went on with their work and did not heed her. So she dragged her half-frozen bare feet again over the cold snow to the edge of Malaga, another island nearby, and managed to attract the attention of the children there. Old Mr. Inger-bredsen came across in his boat and, upon seeing the nature of the tragedy, he called for men from the other islands to bring their guns and they hunted for the maniac, but in vain. At about ten o'clock the "Clara Bella" returned with John Hontvet, Ivan and Matthew, they were stunned by the grue-some sight of their loved ones and were so overcome that two of them swooned, with grief.

Wagner, in keeping with his calculating Teutonic scientific disposition, went to Portsmouth and at half-past seven was at 25 Water Street. He went to the boarding house of Mary Johnson where he ate, changed his clothing, and soon was out of the house again. He sauntered down into the town, purchased some food, and then decided to take a train in to Boston. Reaching Boston, he tried to locate a ship that would take him on and out but this failing as no ship was going out at that time, he again began to walk about. He went to a barber and had his hair trimmed, then to Jacob Todtman, at 39 Fleet Street, where he bought a pair of shoes. From there he went, at about four in the afternoon, to a sailor's boarding house kept by Katharine Brown and her husband at 295 North Street. He held conversation with an Emma Miller in a barroom, and returning to Mrs. Brown's he sat down by the stove and took a nap.

While he was loitering his time away, marking each step of his progress for identification and evidence against him later, the "Clara Bella" had reached the mainland with John Hontvet on board her. The police were notified immediately and, through the information that Hontvet gave the police of Wagner's hide-outs, they telegraphed to Boston, and that same evening the police were at Brown's and Wagner was arrested on the charge of murder.

The next day, with crowds of Boston curiosity seekers which followed him everywhere the officials took him, for the murder was so gruesome in its details that the full feeling of the people was aroused to anger, he was taken back to Portsmouth by train. At Portsmouth there was another large delegation of angry men from the Shoals to greet him and to try to kill him, my father among them. They were stopped only from accomplishing their purpose by a detachment of Marines who had been called out to prevent a riotous hanging.

Several days later, when they were about to transfer Wagner to Saco, Maine, for Smutty Nose was under the jurisdiction of the Maine courts so that Wagner was to stand trial there, my father and two hundred men from the Shoals, Portsmouth, and vicinity, went into Portsmouth again to try to lynch him and to give him the fishermen's personal hanging, but because of the force of the law they were again unsuccessful. Hooting and yelling, wild ejaculations dinned the ears of Wagner way into midnight, the fishermen, in their clumbering fishing boots and waving their old tar ropes, followed the officials to the trains and whenever possible tried to aim at Wagner with a stone or so.

Like all other prisoners or victims of murder mania there were all sorts of theories connected with the murder. While in prison, Wagner acted the usual part of the religious innocent who has been unjustly wronged and he blamed the whole affair on Maren. He claimed that Maren, in a fit of jealous hysteria, had murdered her sisters in cold blood. The courts quickly disposed of this theory with the necessary data of evidence which Wagner had scattered all about him. He was given a fair trial in every manner, and, on June 18th, he was found guilty of murder in the first degree and a year later he was hanged.

Karen and Anethe were buried side by side in the old South Cemetery. A year after the murder of his wife, Ivan Christensen went back to Norway, alone. John and Maren Hontvet moved into Portsmouth, taking the dog with them, and from thereon John Hontvet took up his fishing trawls again, only this time he set out from the mainland where he remained until he died.

When I was a baby, Louis Wagner used to come in and out of our house. My mother has often told me that more than once he held me in his big, brawny arms and cuddled me with his broken English. She always said that he could swear more than any man she had ever heard. His commiting the murder was a surprise to most of the Shoalers, for they had liked and respected Wagner in many ways. While we were living in the house, strangers from the mainland and the cities, looking for souvenirs of the murder, would come and be allowed to cut out pieces, which were still bloodstained, and of the room where the murders were committed. Lem Caswell refused to repair any part of the house, claiming that he was able to make more money by allowing the people to come and see it and by selling the pieces of the house as souvenirs.

The Isles of Shoals was a great busy place in the summers during my boyhood. Between the months of June and September everything was buzzing. The two hotels at Appledore and Star were in full swing. There were two large steamers going back and forth making three round trips a day, and there was a big side-wheel steamer called the "John Brooks" that was running between Boston and the Isles. The steamer "Pinaforte" went from Appledore to Star, from hotel to hotel. There would be many pleasure yachts cruising in and around the shore waters. It was throbbing with life of every kind, the rich, the poor, literate and illiterate, poets and fishermen, realists and idealists, living and working side by side in their appreciation of the beauty and usefulness of these Isles.

There were many noted guests continually walking about and, to catch their attention as children are so apt to do, my sister Jennie and I would go out on the beach and pick up the shells from the rocks. Hour after hour we would sit and string them together and sell them to these guests for fifty cents a string. And as I remember the varied colors and shapes of the shells they were very pretty strings.

Some days I would take the rowboat and go over to Hog

Island (later called Appledore) to help Mr. Oscar Laighton. He was a grand old man, so congenial and kind, and possessing a pleasing personality that would win the heart of any boy. Then he lived at the Appledore house which was in later years burned down flat. It was a very large spacious hotel. Once a week he would come over to our island to see if we wanted to go to Portsmouth in the steamer "Pinaforte." My grandfather would then say: "John, you take the eggs and go in with them."

I would go in the steamer with Mr. Laighton to the mainland and trade the eggs for groceries. The man to whom I traded them was a William Downs. I would get what I wanted on the mainland, and out we would go back to the shoals for another week or more before we would go to the mainland again.

I was a big help to Mr. Oscar as I was young and active. He would let me steer the steamer going and coming to Portsmouth for stores. The people living on the Shoals in those days were as one big family and his sister, Celia Thaxter, was also one of us. I remember that one time I needed to get something from Mr. Oscar. He was not at home but she was. I went to the door and asked her for it. She jokingly pulled my nose and said: "Mr. Oscar to you." She was a grand lady, always remaining the same to everyone.

Was I excited when the Indians came to Star for the summer! They would come from out Bar Harbor way, from the old Indian villages, to make and sell sweet fern baskets to the hotel guests. They pitched their tents over the Island and stayed all summer. I thought they were the greatest persons on earth! I worshipped the very ground that each Brave walked on. To my delight they would make me bows and arrows and taught me how to shoot with them. The Indian children and I got along well together, exchanging customs and words as well as learning each other's methods of play. When the season closed, they would break camp and go back home. I felt real lonesome then. My heroes had left.

Often I would be the only boy out there, but I did not mind it. There was one man there who was my real pal and companion. He was the keeper of the Oceanic Hotel and he and I would go out gunning together all the time. His name was Oliver Frisbee, a college Professor. He was a large fellow and very jolly, with a right good sense of humor.

There was a large fish firm on the Island owned by Lem Caswell, who bought fish from the fishermen and who would cure them. He also ran the only grocery store there, where we children used to buy brown sugar to eat instead of candy. I often went out in a small boat and caught rock codfish, some of them as red as blood, and brought them in and he would buy them of me with dates and candy.

At the age of eleven, my brother Eddie and I were taken by my father to go in the big vessel. After we sighted the fish, two of us went in one small boat together. We thought we were big fellows, then. The vessel was the "White Rover" in which my father was blown off to sea in trying to save two men in a small boat. They were given up for lost. You could not lose a good man in those days. They were made of iron as they used to say, they had iron men and wooden ships; now, it is wooden men and iron ships. They lost the vessel but they were saved. The vessel went ashore on Ipswich Bay.

Later I shipped for four months on a fishing trip along the coast of Maine. We were in and out with trips of fish. The captain was a good man and I liked him. He had a wonderful mother. She took me in as her own boy. She taught me how to sew and while I was staying with her I made a fine patchwork quilt. When the trip was over, and I was coming back, she felt badly and wanted me to stay with her. She had four boys of her own. They had all gone off fishing. Whenever I was in port I always helped her. She had a buffalo cow that I used to milk. It was beginning to seem like home there. In a way I hated to leave to go back home again and to go back to school. I never spent much money as Mr. West Osgere, the captain, kept it for me. And when I reached home I had all of my money, as his mother had sewed it up in my inside pocket. They brought me as far as Portland and sent me home, where I gave all of my money to my mother.

My brother Eddie also went off on a large vessel to the Grand Banks, which is about two hundred miles due east from the States, as the down-easter calls them, off Halifax, Nova Scotia. It was a long trip from four to five months and during this time I was the oldest boy at home. I was growing gaunt and tall at a very fast rate. The different members of the family were beginning to leave one by one. My Uncle Levi had a huge vessel built which he called the "Albert Woodbury." He left the island with his family and went to the mainland. Uncle Oliver moved in to the mainland where he went into the fish business, a retail market, in which enterprise he was very prosperous. That left my brother and I out on the rocks. I was then only thirteen. We continued on as always. In the year following, my Uncle Levi supervised another vessel being built—a great big one which he called after the name of his daughter, "Agnes Downs." She was a beauty. It was all in the family. My father went as captain of the "Albert Woodbury." He then went over to the mainland to live, but not I. I had a cow to milk and a hundred hens to take care of for my grandfather and grandmother. So they all left the island except we three, and I did not leave for a year or so later.

At daylight I could see the old sun come up red as fire. My

grandmother would say: "A hot one today, John." At the age of fourteen I was the only boy on the island. I was the man left to take care of my grandmother and grandfather. Grandmother bought me a new shot gun and with it I would go out back of the Island hunting for ducks. I would take Tig as my companion. Tig was a big, black, Newfoundland dog and was fourteen years old, also. Every duck that I shot, Tig would go and bring it back to me, wagging his tail in glee. He was a great friend, my real pal, but his eyes began to go back on him and he was becoming gradually blind. Sorrowfully, we did away with him and buried him beside a large rock. From then on, things seemed to change. In my mind I had lost my best pal, Tig; then my grandmother being eighty, and my grandfather seventy-nine, they had to decide to move to the mainland where they did not live long afterwards. They were the last of my family to leave the Isles of Shoals behind. The Downs' were one of the first families to come and the last to go.

On the mainland I attended the Haven School. This school is the oldest in the city of Portsmouth, built on South School Street in 1845. This was the first schoolhouse of more than two rooms, and during its construction the voters of Portsmouth denounced the city's extravagance.

Being the tallest boy I would carry the wood up for the fire. These logs were more than two feet long as there was no coal, only wood being used. I was the fireman and the wood-carrier. Interested in all of the sports which the school had, I soon took part. We had a baseball team of all big husky fellows and it took a good team to beat us from the neighboring towns. At sixteen years of age I entered into the bicycle races which were frequently held and won the championship. At eighteen, I became a runner and won one long distance race in the city, during which time I ran an hour without stopping. Rowing the boat was also a sport I enjoyed immensely. On the Fourth of July we had boat races between the men and boys. At the Haven School we had an eight-oar row boat. Other schools would try to compete with our speed but the Haven School generally won the flag.

Fourteen years I spent on the Isles. On them I learned to work and to play—to learn above all to deal with men of all types. Four more of my younger years I spent in Portsmouth, matching my strength with others and acquiring the ability to play fair with life. They were very many happy days, full of activity and observing the sweating of honest men's brows. In later years I found them to be of great value in laying a firm basis for the hardships of everyday living. My young days were not spent without gain.

CHAPTER VIII

LIFE AS A COOK

LIVING ON A vessel out of reach of the comforts of the nineteenth century civilization was a question of special ingenuity, not only on the part of the captain but on the part of the cook. Scientific methods of food preservation were not in use. The amount of the food supply was continually a matter of vast importance and discussion, as there was no definite limit of time in the moving journey of a sailing vessel whose whole momentum depended upon the driving force of the wind. Fishermen out in the open air were ferocious eaters, cuddling appetites which were unknown to the land-lubbers of the shores and their tastes had to be abided by by the wary cook, who generally survived by their good nature. Being a cook on a fishing vessel was certainly a vast responsibility which any man would stagger under, as I found in my experiences as such.

The fishing vessel had fairly good living quarters. There was the forecastle where ten or twelve of the crew lived, and also the cook. Another large compartment, which we called the ice house and where we kept our meat and the fresh food, was next to it. Then came the hole where the ice for the fish was put, and generally fifty tons of ice were stored there. The captain's cabin was in better repair and a little more elaborately furnished and decorated, for which fact it was respected by all of the crew.

In our family we had three large vessels. One was named the "Agnes E. Downs," the others were the "Albert W. Woodbury" and the "Mary E. Caswell." My Uncle Levi Downs was captain of the "Agnes E. Downs," my Uncle Oren Caswell was captain of the "Mary E. Caswell" and my father was the captain of the "Albert Woodbury." As I was growing up, I was a water boy and a cook on the "Albert W. Woodbury." The life on a fishing vessel at that time was an interesting one. If you didn't weaken you would wait for the vessels to go out when the weather would break. You would see about twenty-five or thirty boats going to the fishing grounds—all trying to beat one another to get there first because the first one would get the biggest haul. Year after year we would go and do the same thing over and over. It was one steady grind. It was more work than money, for sometimes you made a great deal of money and then at other times you would get very little. It was all luck and chance, depending on the amount of fish you might catch. On my first trips out in these fishing vessels I was not so much interested in the catching of the fish as I had to be interested in the intricacies of being a cook.

Three-fourths of a cook's life on a fishing vessel was spent in the forecastle. I got up at four o'clock in the morning or even earlier to get the breakfast. The meal hours were at five in the morning, at three o'clock in the afternoon and at ten o'clock at night. When I finished preparing the breakfast I either rang the bell or blew the horn. The men would come in, striding in their large boots and hurrying while sleepingly rubbing their eyes. Down they would sit to plenty of food and really relishing it, as they knew that their day's work was always to be a hard one. It took them about a half-hour to eat. They were great big fellows, most of them being six feet and over. Being very jolly men, they would give and take a joke at any time. If they liked the cook, they would do anything to help him. Sometimes one would say: "Well, Cook, what are you going to have for dinner?" I would answer: "I think a good baked haddock's all right, what do you say, fellows?"

"That suits us," they would respond with enthusiasm.
So I would get two large haddock and cook them. These
suggestions help the cook just as the mother at home, for the
men on a ship's vessel is the cook's family and a big husky
one at that. If they take to the cook it is much easier sailing.

After breakfast was over, they would go out in the boats.
Then the cook was all alone except for the captain. I would
wash the forecastle floor so it would look clean. The rules
were just the same as they were for a home. If anyone threw
a burned match on the floor, he would have to wash the floor,
after I had washed it for the day. The floor was always to be
kept clean at all times.

When all the work for the day was finished, the men would
sit around and play cards. Some read books, some of them
would help me clean up, while some would write back home.
There would be some vessel going home about every day. It
would be some vessel that would stop and ask if there were
any news to exchange or letters to be carried home. The
captain would go aboard with the mail and when they go for
market when bound for home the vessel would fly the stars
and stripes. We would sit around on deck until evening set
in. One by one the men would drop into their bunks to sleep
until the early part of the next morning.

Another responsibility of the cook was to help the captain
in case of emergencies. I would often have to help put the
small boat in the water when the men left the vessel. They
looked for the cook to know a great deal. I remember an
incident when we were coming home from the Grand Banks
on one trip.

It was very thick weather. It was so foggy that we could
not see in front of us. We were nearing land, so I had to be
on the lookout for fear we would make a wrong landing.
All hands were on deck. All at once I heard the lookout

ahead of me yell, "Land ahead!" My brother's voice began roaring through the fog: "Let go the jib."

The jib was the first sail on the vessel. I knew we were near land. My brother then gave the command: "Let go the anchor."

Over went the anchor. The wind was blowing hard and the waves were running high and rough. I heard the cable going and a great deal of grating noise on the deck. This sounded quite unusual, so I rushed to where the commotion was and found that the cable had got away from the crew and they had lost control of it. Something had to be done and right away at that! I grabbed the rope that was lying around there and with a three round turn I stopped the cable and the vessel jerked to a stop not far from land, near the bank side of Cape Cod at Chatham, Massachusetts, a very dangerous spot to be wrecked in.

At one time, I shipped with my Uncle Levi Downs on the schooner "Henry Friend," a big fishing vessel. It was in the Fall of 1892. We went shore fishing in the Ipswich Bay. There we would catch large codfish off Ipswich Bay near Newburyport. We got ready to start out. Upon checking up, we had no cook. The one we had had, was Cookie Benson. He had gone home to visit his family across the ocean in Sweden and he had stayed there. We were ready to start out with no time to hunt up another. I had signed up this time as one of the crew. My uncle was wondering where he could find another cook in such short notice, when he turned to me and said: "John, see if you can't cook until Cookie Benson gets back if he is coming."

At first, I did not want to do it. It took too much of my time. This was a different trip than the other voyage; I was married. I had a family to support, one girl and another child coming, so in order to earn some money I decided to take it.

I cooked until Cookie Benson came home. I let him take his rightful place and I went on the next voyage as a business man and one of the crew. But the crew did not like Cookie Benson's cooking as well as mine and they told me so and wanted me to do it again, but he was a much older man and I liked him so I would not take away his work.

Such was my life as a deep sea cook. It was a trying one. I did not have much spare time having from eighteen to twenty-four men always in my family but, as the housewife or the city baker, my full reward was the hearty compliment of the eater and I beamed with culinary delight when the plates were cleared, knowing that my art had not been spent in vain.

CHAPTER IX

MY WIFE

"When love comes to the harbourmaster
Of a small market town,
It's little he cares for the coastwise ships
Careering up and down.
It's little he cares for freightage rates
Of ridiculous harbour-dues,
And any old craft may sail in or out,
Whenever the captains choose."
                                    —Anonymous.

ROMANCE bursts in upon our lives without giving us much forewarning and then inveigles the rest of our career. Mine was not a Romeo and Juliet courting, nor a whirl of intrigues surrounding a Casanova, it was just the plain, ordinary courtship and marriage of any layman who meets, courts, marries, and then settles down to life. It is the same story that is centuries old and told always in the same language of impressions. But, to me, as an individual mind, it was the most important event.

The settlement of Plymouth and the landing on Plymouth Rock in the winter of 1620, has always been in the annals of American History an event for each to revere and the sturdy stock from which these wanderers came has always been duly praised. Within the twenty years and more following this landing, there were many other Pilgrims of one nature or another who settled along the New England coast of whom there is only bare mention in history. New Hampshire can rightfully boast of its own Plymouth Rock in accordance with the research work contained in the Geneaology of the Odiorne Family:

"The locality which should be the most venerated, not only by our own townsmen, but by every citizen of New Hampshire, is certainly where the first emigrants landed, and the spot where was erected the first house in New Hampshire.

"This place, of so much historic interest, is only about three miles from Market Square; and an hour's walk through interesting scenery will bring you there. We find the name of John Odiorne occupying this locality in 1660. Odiorne's Point should be respected as our Plymouth Rock. Here, in 1623, the little band, who were commissioned by the Laconia Company in England to found a plantation, landed. There are visible remains left to locate the spot where the first house, called Mason Hall or the Manor House, was erected. The well of the house is still to be seen in the field; and the cool fresh water running from beneath the ledge on the shore, scarcely above the tidewater, flows as freely as when Tiwson, the Hiltons, and their companions, quenched their thirst from it two hundred and fifty years ago."

Thus the Odiorne family were among the Pilgrims to settle here. They were descendants of possible French and English origin but more directly have they descended from the English. James Creighton Odiorne, in his geneaology of the family, quotes of its extraction taken from "Ireland's History of Kent" that:

"In the parish of Wittersham, Kent, is a manor called Owlie, anciently written Overley, having had owners of this name, in which family it was vested till the reign of Richard II (1377). It then passed to that of Odiarne, an ancient race of some renown, whose arms are painted on the windows of the north chancel of the church. In this family it continued until the reign of Henry VIII (1529), when Thomas Odiarne appears by his will to have died possessed of the estate. The church of Wittersham is a handsome building, and contains two aisles and two chancels. Near the entrance were the arms and name of Odiarne.

"Though we suppose this family to be of French origin (and this supposition is strengthened by a tradition to that effect) yet we think our immediate ancestors were from England. Their language was English; their customs, habits, proclivities, were English.

"From the preceding records, it will be seen that the name Odiorne has been known in England for about six hundred years. Some families who bore it resided in Oxney, an island in the Rother, a river of Kent, which flows into the British Channel at Rye; others lived in Maidstone and its vicinity; and a few resided in the adjoining shires of Surrey and Sussex. Some of these families were residents in Kent at the time when John Mason in that region formed the Laconia Company, to begin a plantation in New Hampshire; and as our ancestors, but a few years later, settled on the identical spot appropriated for his plantation.

"The first settlers of New Hampshire were generally of that class of merchants denominated, in the reign of Queen Elizabeth, as merchant adventurers. They were active, intelligent, and enterprising men,—men of large views, and strong practical sense and they displayed that unceasing industry, and quickness of resource, which are among the most prominent traits of the commercial character."

So, certain of these facts, the younger Odiorne writes further that: "The line of descent from John Odiorne, extending through eight generations, is nearly perfect, and embraces all of the race in this country."

Of the characteristics of the early Odiornes: "On these points we cannot speak with certainty, except so far as relates to the living race and to the recent dead. With many of those who have passed away during the last half-century, we have had a personal acquaintance; and, of others, there are memorials which help us to form a judgment.

"As far as our observation and acquaintance has extended, we have found them high-minded, self-reliant, energetic, and decided in character, fearless in the expression of their thoughts and feelings, and very little influenced by the frowns and flatteries of the world. They occupy the middle station in life, and manifest little ambition to rise above it. They are, as a class, domestic in their habits, exemplary in their lives, and of religious tendencies. Over and above these traits, through every branch of the family, far and wide, there is apparent an indomitable will, which bears up its possessor, and leaves its impress on the character and life."

Ralph May, in his "Early Portsmouth History" writes of the settling of Odiorne's point: "As arranged in the agreement, Thomas sailed in the ship 'Jonathan' in the late winter or early spring of 1623, and arrived, probably in April or early May of that year, off the mouth of the Piscataqua River. Thomson took his men ashore at what is now Odiorne's Point, on the outer edge of what is now known as Little Harbor, as 'fitt place to build their houses for habitacons.' Probably because this point was a part of what was, at high tide, an island of about six hundred acres in area."

The first one of whom note was made was John Odiorne who "was born about 1627; died at New Castle, New Hampshire in 1707. It is not known in what year this ancestor came to America. On the 13th January, 1660, a division of public lands was made at Portsmouth, N. H., among those who were inhabitants there in 1657; and to John Odiorne a grant was made of forty-two acres on Great Island lying at the entrance harbor. A few years later he received a second grant, which probably included that section of land at the mouth of the Piescatqua River which has since been known as Odiorne's Point."

Two hundred and twenty years ago, in about the year 1720, the Honorable Jotham Odiorne, a member of his Majesty's council, lived in New Castle and carried on business enterprises in Market Square in Portsmouth. He was, as well, the manager and owner of a large number of fishing vessels. He married a Mehitable, one of the daughters of Robert Cutt of Kittery. He had a reasonably large family that married into the Appleton, Hart, and Pearse and Treadwell families. He was a man of shrewd temperament and of colonial English dignity.

In 1767 there is a record of Jack Odiorne, the sheriff, who punished a negro slave at the town pump by giving him a lashing. The story as given from "Brewsters' Rambles In Portsmouth" is as follows:

"If any black was guilty of any crime which was regarded disgraceful to the society, he was duly tried and punished. Nero's viceroy was Willie Clarkson, a slave of Hon. Peirse Long. A report comes that Prince Jackson, slave of Nathaniel Jackson of Christian Shore, had stolen an axe. The sheriff, Jock Odiorne, seizes him, the court is summoned, and King Nero in majesty sits for the examination. The evidence is exhibited, Prince is found guilty, and condemned to twenty lashes on the bare back, at the town pump on the parade. There was a general gathering of the slaves on such occasions and the sheriff, after taking off his coat and tying up the convict to the pump, hands the whip to his deputy, Pharaoh Shores, addressing the company, "Genmen, this way we s'port our government"—turning to his deputy—"Now, Pharaoh, pay on!" After the whipping was over, the Sheriff dismissed the prisoner, telling him that the next time he is found this side Christian Shore, unless sent by his master, he will receive twenty lashes more. Prince, however, did not reform; for, soon after, he was found guilty of larger thefts and brought under the cognizance of the county court."

Thereby, in scanning the records of early life in Portsmouth, one can find the name of Odiorne scattered throughout its happenings. On March 15, 1889, I married into the Odiorne family. My wife's mother was a Miss Dorothy Odiorne, descending from the Odiorne family who lived in Portsmouth during Indian times. Her father was the late Horace Spinney, a native of Eliot, Maine. The Spinney family also dates back to Indian stories and the name of Spinney dots the early history of Portsmouth.

At about 1659, there was a Thomas Spinney who owned land on Eliot Neck in Maine. Later Margaret Waterhouse's and Samuel Brewster's daughter, Mary, married Mr. Spinney, "a ship carpenter." Brewster writes at length about the Spinney family.

"It has been thought that Neptune had only an existence in heathen mythology—but fifty years ago there was a personage here who so nearly resembled the fabled sea king, that he bore the name. 'Old Neptune' and 'Cap Spinney' were the names given to John Spinney, a veteran of the Revolutionary stock, who became of age in the time of the old war.

"It is said that Thomas Spinney was the first of the name who came to this country from England, about two hundred years ago. He settled in Eliot, on the spot now occupied by Wentworth Fernald. About thirty years after, Joseph Spinney took up his residence at Spinney's Neck on the river. They were some months residents before one day Joseph, in an excursion in the woods, called at a house for refreshments. They found in the course of conversation that they were of the same name, and that they were brothers! Thomas had left home when Joseph was an infant, who knew not in what part of the country his brother had located. From Thomas Spinney the families of Thomas and Joseph Spinney in this city descended. Our 'Neptune' was a descendant of the first Joseph, and lived on the family homestead.

"We knew Cap Spinney many years, and time and again witnessed his arrival and departure from the spring market. He was portly in person, upright in posture, of dark skin, long beard, and was invariably clad in petticoat trousers, and a pea-jacket so covered with patches of every color that it was a matter of doubt what was the original—a blue knit cap was drawn close to his head, and red edging and ear pieces turned up around. His adhesion to this cap gave him the above designated name. He was a man of system and independence, and his routine for business was strictly adhered to. He would leave his home at Eliot at any hour between midnight and daylight that the tide served, and alone in his canoe proceed to the mouth of the river. When the tide required him to leave before he had finished his sleep, on reaching the fishing grounds he would bait his hooks, giving one turn of his line around the tholepins, and then another turn around his wrist, compose himself to sleep. When the fish bit, the check at the tholepin would secure it, and the slight pull at his wrist would notify him to take it in. He would then rebait, redrink, and continue his nap,—and in due time he might be seen coming up the river and rowing into the market landing. To the calls, 'Have you any fish?' no reply would be made. As soon as his painter was fastened, he would raise his cuddy cover, take out his cocoanut shell, visit a particular shop near the market, get it filled with 'be-joyful,' then return to his boat, take his seat, raise his cocoanut to his mouth and take two or three swigs, resting between each with a smack of his lips—then depositing it safely in the cuddy, he uncovers his fish and gives notice, 'Now, Gentlemen, I am ready for business.' By the time the fish were sold, his shell would need replenishing, and then with another swig he would push off into the stream, and his boat proceed almost intuitively to his home. Thus year after year he went through the same routine, until in 1832, on the 4th day of July—a day which he struck against Portsmouth Bridge, and at the age of 73 he regarded as worth a particular observance in his way, his boat closed his life in that river in which he had almost lived for three-score and ten years. He left about fifteen hundred dollars as the results of his labors, and the reputation of a friendly disposition to man and beast, as well as to his cocoanut shell. His like we have never since looked upon."

As to whether or not this Spinney was a relative of my wife I have not been able to find out. Names or family descent did not mean anything to me when I married. I was overjoyed. I had married a girl named Josephine, which to me was the prettiest name possible. At least, I thought so, and to me she was one of the prettiest. She was an angel in my eyes. My wife was then fifteen years old and I, nineteen, when we married.

I was far older in words. I had been brought up to do big things on that big farm, the Atlantic Ocean, that was what I called it. From our wedding day on until she passed away we worked together. I always said that the two greatest things in my life were my wife and the old ocean.

We began housekeeping on the little that I was able to earn. I went fishing in the summer and in the winter I would work in the Brass Foundry where I earned fifteen cents per hour, six days a week, working ten hours per day. My weekly salary became seven dollars and a half. Nevertheless, we were satisfied and worked together to get through to Spring when I would make big money by going fishing. My wife and I would work night and day sometimes to bait my fishing gear, she would cut bait way into the night. I would bait the hooks for the next day and off I would go at about two o'clock in the morning out to sea for a day's catch, which would sometimes more than pay me and sometimes not. It was always the same—more than enough or not enough. It went on. The children came and we became one happy family. We did not get very far ahead, but we had about all we wanted. On the twenty-fourth of November, 1892, our boy was born. He was a big fellow of ten pounds. This livened us up and we worked all the harder. We thought the world was working with us.

We worked on for many years with always the dream of owning our own little home. At the age of forty years, with what we had scraped together, we bought a little home of our own. It was not a newly built home but it was a home that we could claim. We had all we could care for with twelve children, four boys and eight girls.

On the fifteenth of March, 1939, we reached the golden mile-stone together, after having traveled a difficult road being borne up happily with each other's support. We celebrated our Golden Wedding Anniversary with great pomp and ceremony, amidst the music and laughter of children and grandchildren. My wife never seemed so contented, happy and beautiful as then, and little I realized how soon after we were to be parted.

She passed away at the age of sixty-six on the sixth day of August of that year. We had not been destined to continue on much further than the golden milestone. She had stopped off at the roadside and I had to go on alone, even though my footsteps becomes heavier with each new step. I have trudged on, lonely and unable to forget the wife who had brightened and spurred on the way for me. I have traveled but it has been of no avail, I have been to one place of recreation after another but I have not enjoyed them, so I have gone back to the home again, but it seems empty. Even lobstering has lost its appeal, and a new car is but an object to be used. I am unable to forget my wife.

My life, however, has been prosperous with those happy years spent back in the eighties. I have not had millions but I have lived evenly and had everything I wanted. And now I am spending alone a new cycle with a sacred memory forever present in my dreamings.

CHAPTER X

SWORDFISHING

SWORDFISHING is one of the most dangerous and fascinating forms of fishing. As a sport it is thrilling, but as a business it is treacherous. Swordfishing is a matter of hard muscular skill and brawny salt-water strength in the hurling of the iron. It is a matter of a quick eye and steady nerve in hauling the swordfish aboard vessel without injury to anyone on the vessel. The fish is well named, and its sword is mighty.

The life that swordfishing man begun was late in the month of June, on or about the twentieth. The season was very short. Sometimes we would set sail for the fishing grounds off Nantucket Sound, fifteen miles from the mouth of Vineyard Sound, and from there we would go to Block Island, Rhode Island, which is off Newport about twelve miles out in the direction of the southwest. We would cruise for days looking for swordfish. Other times we would not get any fish until July and then you would have to go to the Grand Banks and Georges (a hundred miles from the Grand Banks off Halifax). We have followed from time to time in the swordfish business and have made a great deal of money, but the season was short and we had to catch many in order to balance our profits in such time.

Often our trips were very hard ones. A regular swordfisherman has to go off shore and lay in wait for the weather in order to catch them, and many have been the hours that we have waited for a catch. Swordfish are not always seen in the roughest of weather. They are apt to show up in very moderate weather and when the sun is fully out. On a good hot day the swordfish can be sighted a good ways off because he is a long ways out of the water. On a rough day he just shows the ends of his fins, whereas on a good calm day his fin is all out. The way to tell a swordfish from a shark is that a swordfish shows two fins and a shark shows one in the distance. Swordfish very often go in schools. Generally one or two may be caught, and then you have to sail for miles before you see any more. I never saw but one school of swordfish and that day we got sixteen in the forenoon before they settled down. Swordfish naturally come to the top of the water about midday. Late in the afternoon they go down again and sometimes they may be seen again about sundown. All fish, in a way, come to the top of the water—more so at sundown and just before the sun rises in the morning.

A swordfish does not see much coming right head on. He sees more of what is coming in back of him. In chasing him we would not try to come up back of him but would always try to meet him coming head on.

We would cruise for days looking out for them. After a while, sometimes hours and sometimes days, we would see some in the distance but the weather was too windy and we could not catch up with them that day but we chased them on the next. We caught ten swordfish that day. We had no motor power to speed our vessels at our will, we could only catch them at the will of the wind for we had to depend entirely on the sails, but in those days we knew no difference and did not mind these delays. We just went with the wind. We would get a few every day, so that after a short time we would get enough to go to the market.

Sighting the swordfish was simple but the most difficult part was the catching of him. A member of the crew stood on the bow of the boat with a pole with an iron dart at the end with a three-foot line. When he got within striking distance of the swordfish, he would put the dart right through the fish. Then came the dreaded struggle. Out in the liner is a half barrel with the line around it. The man will throw the barrel overboard into the water. The swordfish will dive toward the bottom of the ocean until he strikes the bottom and then the small boat will be put out to go after him. The men in the small boat would take in the barrel into the boat and start to pull in the line. If the fish is struck in the wrong spot he will fight the line or rope and follow it back; so that if you do not watch out he will come right through the boat.

I had one thrilling experience. I ironed a swordfish one day. He was only a small one weighing about one hundred and fifty pounds. He was struck right through the middle and was he wild! I had to throw the dart at him again. The small boat went out after him. They were new at it, just having joined the crew this trip, so they did not understand what to do with the oncoming furious fish and before they had a chance to decide what to do or to get away the fish, with all of his might, put his sword right through the dory between one of the men's legs. The men did not realize what was happening until my father, the Captain, for it was on the "Albert Woodbury" yelled: "Hold on to that sword!"

This they did with all of their frightened strength. We got to them with the vessel and secured hold of the fish. We killed him and hauled him aboard the vessel. These men never forgot this experience. In spite of this freak accident we caught sixteen swordfish and I was the striker with the iron.

On another trip out we saw a bird of a fish. We were near land while chasing him. He was a wise one. We followed him for hours and hours on end. He was large and it was the last of the season. They ran generally quite a bit larger in the Fall. Finally, after a hot pursuit, we caught up to him. I ironed him. I'll never forget the moment before I was ready to strike. My father called out: "Put it right through him!"

I watched for my chance while catching my breath, and with the full weight of my body, I jabbed it down near his big fin which is on his back. I cut his backbone in two. He became raging. He fought the vessel and put his sword right into the keel. It broke off in the keel. After a frantic struggle for minutes we got him aboard the vessel. He weighed five hundred and fifty pounds. We had to sail into Gloucester to have the part of the sword taken out of the keel. When the sword was out we found it had gone in about four inches. This hole, if it had not been repaired, would have proven dangerous for, when we hooked mackerel, we would haul them up alongside in schools. Then when we set the seine or net around the vessel it would became caught and tear in a hole in the keel.

Swordfishing was great and I enjoyed every bit of it. It was dangerous, but of that type of danger that made a man feel mightier than the forces of Nature; made him feel as though the diversities of life could be ironed and hauled ashore after a struggle and met with, a feeling that is seldom forgotten—a confidence that is injected within his soul to last forever.

CHAPTER XI

MACKEREL MOMENTS

MOONLIGHT on the ocean has been written and painted up in all forms of artistic glory. The clear sky overhead, the myriads of stars blinking out from the vault, the ocean flashing back the path of the moonbeams as a silver mirror, the quiet lisping sounds of the waves as they so seriously lapped the sides of the vessel, have been framed in many ways. Yet there is nothing more beautiful to be seen, fireflying through this blue green picture of the ocean, than the shining flashes of the schools of mackerel on a moonlight night. To stand on the bow of the vessel and to see thousands of these shining phenomena popping in and out of the water, is a vivid image often impressed. I was in all kinds of fishing along the New England coast and mackerel fishing was one of the most entertaining; for of the many fish that I have caught they seemed to have been the most beautiful, the most agile, and the most slippery.

The season for mackerel fishing was from the first of June to the first of November. We started out in the spring on about June the first and sailed for the south to meet the mackerel. We kept sailing due south until we would meet the mackerel.

We used to fish in these southern waters for a while during the mackerel season and as it became warmer we kept moving northward. About the fourth of July we would get them off the Isles of Shoals, and from then on it was a continual cruising from the coast of Maine to the coast of Massachusetts, back and forth from one end of the summer to the other. This was the fishing grounds for the mackerel. The mackerel would spawn and stay there all summer and in the fall we had to follow them back the same way as they had come. The way a fish comes in is the way he goes back. They come north in the spring and go back south in the fall. We would follow them south to around Block Island and then we would lose sight of them. No one knew where they went until the next summer when we would go and hunt them up and would meet them again coming up from the Jersey coast off Cape Henry, which was the first place you would meet them of any account.

Sometimes mackerel are very wild to catch. I have seen them make us set our seines seven times in one day and we would not get a fish. They would dive under our seines every time. Other times they would be so tame that you could row right alongside and get them with ease; usually, it was no easy task. It was all work and you had to know your business. Some mackerel are small and easy to catch, the larger ones are more difficult.

Mackerel fishing was technically exciting. We had a member of the crew at the mast head at the top of the mast, looking around to see if he could sight the mackerel. The mackerel would come to the top of the water and they would form black spots with their heads out. It would be different from any other objects on the water and it would be blacker than anything else. When the man at the mast head yelled out: "School on the port bow!"

We would all hurry and get into the boats, twelve of us in one boat, and row to where the mackerel were. For mackerel fishing these boats are called dories and were used to haul in the trawls.

Nature has made the mackerel so very acute that you have to chase them and in doing so have to get ahead of them. In order to get ahead of them you have to get your seine or large net and keep ahead, and as you turn you have to go around the heads of the mackerel and give them room to move up in. Two boats would go around them in opposite directions until they would come together. Both men would then get into one boat and begin to pull the first line that encircled the seine on the bottom through rings and would draw it together at the bottom so that it became closed and all hands would pull in the seines from the different quarters or boats until the seine was brought to form a bag, and then you would pull all the mackerel that were in the seine into one place and with a large net you would pull them on board the vessel. The seine would have to be reoverhauled ready for another set-out again when the man at the head of the mast would shout: "Another school of mackerel!"

My experiences as a mackerel fisherman were many. Some remain outstanding while others gradually have faded away. I remember that on the night of August 15, 1889, we started from Portsmouth with a load of mackerel for Boston. We put out to sea in the afternoon and just before dark a sinister puff of wind came up and carried off the mainmast. The sea in the hands of this squall became rough and choppy. We thought we would never see a thing again for we were running mountain high on the water. All night long we went up and down not knowing where the vessel was taking us. In the morning we put up a signal. It was not sighted. My father, becoming uncertain about help arriving from some chance passing ship, took two of the men, lowered a dory and rowed to Rockport for help and a steamer came out and towed us. We immediately got a new mast and went right out fishing again.

We were off Newport once trying to make harbor. The wind was so strong we had our sails blown right off the ropes. We let the vessel go with the wind until we could get some of the sails fixed. After the wind had died down, we were a good many miles off our course, way out to sea. It was not as it is today. Help could not be got by sending an S.O.S. by telegraph or radio nor could the mainlanders be contacted in any way. You had to depend upon the behavior of the wind entirely to get you back from where you were going. This was way back in 1888, not much to do but to wait patiently for God's power to get you there. We were then in the mackerel fishing off Block Island. We would catch a trip's load and then go to Newport for market. It was the nearest port to the fishing grounds so we had to wait and do the next best thing we could in getting in and out the harbor. Finally, we made our way to the port and sailed into the harbor safely.

Often mackerel fishing was a quiet life. We would cruise for days without seeing one mackerel. One week went by without sighting one mackerel, when suddenly you would see mackerel all around you and you would be laying off without much wind. I remember we were cruising in the lower part of Maine for mackerel. We had been days without sighting any. Our food was getting low and we would soon have to make harbor, when a big tow boat came along and stopped. The captain yelled out that while coming through the bay he had spotted plenty of mackerel in the night.

Sometimes you can catch mackerel in the night when you are unable to in the day time. A mackerel at night shows up like little balls of fire. They are easier to catch at that time. They don't take any notice of you and you are able to get around them and haul them in quickly.

So after hearing this, we turned around and went back to where the captain of the steamer had directed us which was at Rockland Bay, Maine. At about nine o'clock that night, we ran into the school of mackerel. We had no ice but we loaded the boat with the mackerel and started for Portland, Maine.

The weather was very calm so it took us all day until the next night to get into Portland harbor. When we arrived the mackerel were nearly all spoiled. We lost a great deal of money, because mackerel were high in those days and we had to sell these to the canners for little or nothing. We only got about five cents a pound, where if we had got in with them with plenty of ice and the right refrigeration, we would have got fifteen cents a pound. We had about twenty thousand pounds of mackerel on board. Then the season was getting late, so my father decided to come home and that was the end of the mackerel season for that year. So we went home and started to prepare to go fishing for codfish in Ipswich Bay. It took about a month to change over for codfish as all new lines and equipment had to be rehauled or bought.

The life of a fisherman is a life to be proud of. You can't form a good fisherman. It has to be born in you some way or another. In my days I have taken an interest in some young fellow. It is the same as in any other trade. They start out all right and as long as you are around to look out after them, everything runs smoothly, but they don't last long at it. Fishing is a job that you can not slack up on. It is one of the biggest lotteries in the working world. You have to have skill and a great deal of patience as well as endurance. You might go after fish today, you may find them and you may not. If you are a born fisherman you take it the way it comes. You do not get discouraged. It is your manner of working for a living and you have to get fish in order to live on. It may be days; it may be weeks; but it is your job and you have to stick to it, no matter how hard you have it. On these mackerel fishing trips, my father would take me away from the others and ask confidentially: "Do you think that there ought to be some fish around here?"

"Well," I would say, "I think there is."

"Well, Son," he would always answer, "I want you to know what every good fishing man knows that if the fish were there the year before, he knows that they will be there this year."

I wanted to go into the harbor for the night so that I could go home. So we went. We remained there until the next day taking on more supplies for a long trip down the coast of Maine. There was no wind and we were all day trying to get out of the harbor. Finally we were out in the afternoon and started down the coast. We expected to stay out all night so that we could be down the coast a ways as it was getting dark around sundown. We were off York harbor. We did not think of mackerel. All hands were sitting around on deck—when the lookout cried: "Captain, there's a school of fish off port bow!"

All hands were on their feet in a minute. It did not look like a big school. The day before we had cruised about all day without sighting anything. We all got ready in a rush and went pell-mell after the mackerel. The mackerel were going around and around in circles as they often do. When the bait is around they are very tame. We set the seine around them as they were becoming more tame. It was a sight. They came to the top of the water inside the seine and filled it full. It was an immense haul and after getting them aboard we iced them down. We worked from sundown until sunrise to take care of them. I well remember I chopped ice all that night. It was worth the trouble, for with one hundred eighty barrels of mackerel we went to market.

A fisherman never gets discouraged if he doesn't get a good catch, from one day he thinks of the next day. The day will always come. "It is not what you get today it is what you will get tomorrow," is the fisherman's motto. Thus we kept on trying day after day. One day during the World War schools and schools of mackerel came right to the mouth and harbor of the Piscataqua River. The submarine torpedoes and mines had driven them inshore. I caught five hundred dollars worth of fish in twenty-one days. It is no "ill wind that will not blow in good."

The moments that I spent in mackerel fishing are precious in my memory. They seemed to have passed by very quickly in my retrospect of time but in their fleeting presence I felt many pangs of joy.

CHAPTER XII

CODFISHING IN THE YEAR 1900

TRAVELING through the waters from the northern and temperate seas of Europe to Asia and America and even journeying as far south as Gibraltar, exploring the bottoms of the ocean beds for their meals of worms, mollusks, or smaller, less fortunate fellowmen, are the codfish, voracious and crafty residents of the deep. The most important codfishery in the world is that part of the coast along the Newfoundland Banks where tales have been told of fishermen who have caught over five hundred in ten or eleven hours with hook and lines. These codfish, salted and dried, have been shipped to all corners of the globe, for many valuable products come from the cod. Isinglass has been made from the swimming bladder, and the liver provides the cod liver oil which was used in the nineteenth century for rheumatics and pulmonary consumption and is used today for its nutritive value, for it adds to the body's store of fat and enriches the blood with red corpuscles. The Norwegians have given cod heads to their cows for food, the Icelanders gave the vertebrae, the ribs, and the bones to their cattle and in many places on the desolate steeps of the icy sea the dried bones are used for fuel. Codfish are utilized and known the world over.

As an article of food the codfish is more popular and in better condition for eating the three months preceding the Christmas season. The codfish spawns in February and is a very prolific fish, the roe of a single female has been known to have contained upwards of eight million ova and to form more than half the weight of the entire fish. As in all beings of nature, the rule of the survival of the fittest applies so that by the time eggs are destroyed or eaten, or the small cod are gulped by larger prey, this large number of ova does not increase the quantity of cod to any too great an extent. Large quantities of roe, also, were used in France at one time as ground-bait in the sardine fishery, while in some foreign countries it was used as food in much the same style as caviar. The young are about an inch in length by the end of spring, but cannot be carried into market until the end of the second year, and they reach maturity by the end of their third year. They measure about three feet in length, and weigh usually from twelve to twenty pounds although there have been some caught which weigh from fifty to seventy pounds.

At the end of the mackerel year we began to prepare to go after the codfish. Codfishing, at that time, was also a serious and enterprising business for the fishermen, as the expense of the necessary gear was extraordinary and the catch had to be large to be profitable. The big cod would come off Newburyport in plentiful numbers, and they would stay all winter and then return to where they came from when the spring broke. Those were the days of the great fishing off the coast of Ipswich Bay.

Fifty vessels would start off about the first of November and fish through the winter months in Ipswich Bay. Some of these vessels were large and some were small. The larger vessels had from fourteen to sixteen men on board. There would be about twelve small dories for the larger vessels and from six to ten for the smaller ones. Each dory carried four tubs of trawls. Each trawl would have five hundred hooks, which had to be very strong and heavy. Herring was then used for bait. Out of one herring we would make four to six pieces of bait. One piece of bait was put on each hook. All the trawls would be got ready and set out with one man manning each dory. We would drop them one by one at measured distances apart and all would extend in the same direction. When all the trawls were dropped out, the vessel picked up the small boats and packed them on deck six on each side and when this was done, away we would go home for the night.

On the next day we would go out again and take the fish off the hooks and rehook on new bait and again leave them in the same way. This procedure was repeated again and again day after day.

The fish we caught were generally all large fellows weighing from fifteen to ninety pounds. I have caught some cod weighing over a hundred pounds, but it was very seldom that this happened. The largest one I ever did see was one weighing one hundred and thirteen pounds, which was a rare catch. They appear very nicely in the boat. Each boat would hold from fifty to sixty of them. The females came into Ipswich Bay to spawn and lay their eggs during the cold winter weather. The cold did not affect them in any way and the colder the winter was the closer the fish swam in to shore. Every catch did not prove to be small but profitable.

At Portsmouth, on shore, there were ten main codfish buyers. The principal and best known one was Elvin Newton and Son. He would buy the cod from the fishermen and ship them off to Canada. He would go with them once a week. There would be shiploads and shiploads of cod—a hundred boxes at a time—and at Christmas time I have seen hundreds of boxes on the wharf waiting for the market to rise in price before they were shipped to the markets.

In the spring when the cod that remained went back to their spring resorts the haddock would begin to come into Ipswich Bay the same way. The same vessels would then equip again in the same old way and set out after the haddock. These vessels would return with loads of haddock. Haddock were very easy to catch, but there was always more work to care for them after they were caught. They would have to be carried to the Boston market to be sold. The wind being our only power, this trip would often be a long one and practically a complete loss.

Codfishing was some adventure in the old days. It was cold, hard work in icy gales and sleet-frozen vessels. If the weather were rough the man, alone in the dory, had to use all his strength and skill to manage the oars to keep it balanced top the crest of the wind driven crests. Frozen hands handling cold iron hooks, frozen feet pacing wave swept decks, frozen faces trying in vain to peer through the clear, piercing snowy squalls were just a few of the trials of the codfisherman as he went back and forth for his daily living.

CHAPTER XIII

LOBSTERING

I HAVE BEEN in the lobster business—wholesale and retail for the last fifty years. People come from the old towns from all around and get lobsters right from the ocean caught by my boats and my family. My father retired from deep water fishing. He and I began the business which I have continued to follow. My first lobster market was founded on Mechanic Street in Portsmouth. Later I moved to Union Street and then to Marcy Street where I am now situated.

Fifty years ago my father and I sold lobsters for eight and ten cents apiece. They had to be ten and a half inches long no matter how large (the largest lobster that I ever caught was seventeen and a half pounds). In the early days when we had no power; we thought nothing of rowing a boat eight to ten miles and hauling in from sixty to one hundred lobster pots and rowing back again. Now we have the power to haul the pots. In the years gone by, we had to locate our own bait. Now, we have it brought to us. Even in the rough process of lobstering, science has made it much easier.

The lobster has a life of crude fierceness and varied savagery. About November, the first in the fall, the lobster leaves the rocks and goes off for the winter. During the winter you do not catch many lobsters except if the winter weather is very mild. If it is exceedingly cold you may catch some. They go off shore into deep water and they don't move much in the winter because the cold weather affects the bottom of the ocean as well as the top and so the lobsters hide away for the winter. They leave their rocks to go on the muddy bottom. The muddy bottom does not hold the frost as the rocks; and when in the mud, they do not move around much.

The lobsters do not move very much until in the spring about the month of April. Then a few more are caught increasing in number each day, until about the middle of May. May has been considered the best month for lobstering for years, but at the present time, it is not proving so. The lobsters come in the month of June and if the weather is cold, quite a few may be caught, but, if the weather is very hot and muggy, there is a very short season. The hotter the weather the quicker the lobster will shed his shell.

They will go under the rocks for about three weeks and finally they will come out gradually. One is caught that has shed its shell this week, and one by one they keep coming out until about the middle of August, when the lobsters begin to grow plentiful and from then on you have a good catch of lobsters. Their shells grow hard very quickly. You will haul up a lobster pot and think that you have caught two lobsters, but instead you have not caught any that you can take out of the pot. The lobster that was in this pot has shed his shell. One of the objects in the pot will be shell and the other, the lobster. This lobster may not be taken out because he is very soft. He will have to left alone for a few days until his shell is hard enough so that he may be taken out of the pot.

In the meantime, you will catch a great many lobsters all ready to shed, that we call "black" lobsters because before they shed they are all black—the meat is black and the lobsters look all black. Their shells are often cracked along the back and in that case, care had to be taken if one is caught. When we catch one we place him in a separate compartment in our "lobster car" where it may shed its shell. If we should leave these type of lobsters in with the others and they shed their shells, the live lobsters would eat them up. That is the reason that they are separated and are fed and left in the compartment until their shells are hard enough and ready for market.

A lobster grows once and that is when he sheds. When he is in the process of shedding, he grows about an inch. Now days, a very small lobster before he sheds becomes a market lobster after he has shed. A lobster, after he is shed, has a very watery and flabby soft meat. You are not able to get much out of him after boiling. However, before he sheds, you get the best lobster meat because he is full of meat and better to eat.

It is a peculiar and intricate procedure that the lobster pursues to crawl out of his shell. It is an instinctive and convulsive process and he wiggles his way out of a break in the membrane between his tail and his back. He rolls on his side and kicks his legs vehemently and then he casts his shell. Each molting of the lobster is called a stage in his life. He ordinarily casts four times in the first twelve days of his life and thereafter he molts periodically once a year. The lobster is helped out in this process by the segmentation of his muscles and by his blood-circulation which is lowered considerably. The newly shed lobster is always very shiny and smooth and lifeless. Hard shells are not grown back on again for from six to eight weeks but these shells are helped to be formed by the lobster eating his discarded shell and thereby absorbing the lime.

The female lobsters are of all sizes. I have caught some nine inches long and full of eggs weighing ten pounds in size. Female lobsters begin laying eggs at the age of four to six years and at a size from seven to twelve inches. These eggs are laid at the period of two years apart. The eggs form inside their bodies as a large red substance and some people like to buy them in this condition for they prefer the taste of the lobster. During the later stage of the laying the mother lobster holds her eggs under the tail. These eggs are very large little black specks and when they hatch they turn pink with large eyes. She hides these eggs under the seaweed and rocks, for the male lobster if he should come across them would eat them up. So the eggs disappear beneath moss and rock until they, if they have survived, are able to crawl out.

The period of spawning is from the middle of July to the last of August. After the female lobster has spawned she is not much good. She falls away gradually and months afterwards there is hardly enough meat on her for anyone to eat. I have caught from thirty to forty of them during a season. A seven pound lobster is estimated to hatch about thirty thousand eggs. I have tried to hatch lobster eggs in my own lobster car instead of throwing them away. I would bring them home and put them in the cars and feed them. Later they would hatch. Many times when I have lifted up my lobster car door, the door has been solid full of small lobsters.

After the lobster has laid her eggs and they have become movable, they look like large fleas—they seem to be all eyes. Soon they become noticeable as having the form of the lobster. I never could understand just how fast a lobster grows, not ever having a suitable place with which to experiment. The Bureau of Fisheries have made a study along these lines and from their research the average size of a lobster at one year is two and one-eighth inches, and at ten years, four months the female is twelve inches. Science too claims that it takes a year and a half for a lobster to grow an inch and a half. He has to be from three years to three and a half years old to be a marketable lobster which would be four and three-eighths inches in size. A lobster is measured for market by the length of his back, from the end of his nose to the end of the tail. You are never able to tell the age of a lobster by the size. Lobsters may be caught that are nice and smooth and then

Lobster Cars

My Cat and I taking out lobsters.

The Downs Store

The Author and His Store

A Big Fellow

My son, Teddy, taking out lobsters. The car is beside him.

smaller ones may be caught that are rough and black. There is no way of finding out which is the older. Some lobsters weighing three pounds would be nice and shiny while others would be rough and black. Which would be the older, the smaller or the larger, I have never been able to make out.

The way of catching these lobsters is more or less individualistic work. We build our own lobster pots. They are from thirty-two inches to thirty-six inches long being two feet in width and fourteen inches in height. It is almost a square framed pot, as we call it. It has three bows or frames that are lathed up all around and a door is mode on top. It is closed up on both ends with a head made of twine on the inside of the middle of the pot resembling an old fashioned sand dial that one turns unside down each hour. A head is a bag knitted out of twine and has four corners. It is placed in the square and extended in the pot with a five and a half inch hoop for lobsters to enter. It spreads back about fifteen inches with a hoop about six inches in circumference and is tied up with twine and this we call the "bedroom." In the front end of the pot which is smaller we have a head on each side that ties in the pot about six inches with a hoop on the inside that we leave open about four inches apart. A lobster enters these side heads. The bait hangs between them. The lobster goes in to eat and instead of going out the side head, he crawls through the bedroom head and drops down to the bottom of the pot and the trap has then sprung. That is the manner in which we catch them. After the lobster drops down into the lobster pot he's there for awhile for he has to puzzle out how to get out of the pot which is not an easy task.

These lobster pots are hauled very early in the morning, generally hauled in once a day. The lobster is a sneak. He does most of his roaming about during the blackness of the night. Some lobsters can not make up their minds to go into the bedroom part so they stay on the outside part and as soon as daylight comes they go out again. I have baited my pots at daylight and to show you how slyly intelligent a lobster is and how they get out are the evidence that they have been, and left, after having baited my pots at daylight and hauled the lobster pots up again. Later on I have gone back and rehauled them to find that the lobsters have been at the bait, proving that they go in sometimes in the daytime and cleverly find their way out again.

Caring for the lobsters after they have been caught is another serious problem of the lobster fisherman. For this purpose, we have large lobster cars in which to put them and to hold them. While living in these cars they have to be fed the same as you would feed chickens. They are fed with the same bait as is used to catch them. They eat all kinds of fish, especially fresh fish. These cars are boxes ranging from the size of a room to the size of a box. They are about forty by sixty or smaller, being made from pine or spruce boards and dropped about three feet deep into the water. They have to be dropped fairly deep so that the cold will not kill the lobsters.

It is work to car them up for so many are caught every day. They have to be carefully watched for if any should die, they have to be taken out. If the dead lobsters are not removed, the live lobsters will eat them up and at times they are so cannibalistic that they even eat live ones also. A lobster is very ferocious when he is hungry. He will eat any kind of fish at that time. A lobster in the ocean is not able to see much. He scents his food and the more the fish smells the more he likes it; and, if it is used for bait the more lobsters you are likely to catch. I have seen lobsters on the bottom that would never go into a trap. It is Nature's rule that you only catch on an average of ten out of a hundred lobsters that are around where you have your traps. It must be so for if it were not there would not be any there the next day. You are able to catch just so many of all kinds of fish. Thousands of fish may be seen around and if they are in the midst of hook and line, only one would probably be caught out of the thousand.

Lobsters are the same. Not all that are around are caught. The lobster is very foxy. Sometimes a lobster will be in a pot and after you have hauled him aboard the boat, he is so lively that two claws are in the air all the time trying to get you. You have to bother and get him on his back before he has a chance to bite. He likes the shade in the daylight. He will go for the first dark spot he is able to see on the bottom of the ocean or in the lobster car, and hide himself away. Some think that the lobster is easy to catch but in my day I have found out that they are just as particular and intelligent as the days are long.

A lobster when he is moving fast never crawls, he drives himself by the flap of his tail. He travels at a good rate of speed. One flap of his tail and he advances many feet for I have tried to catch him many times. He is hard to keep alive after you put him in the car. I have lost eighty lobsters in one night out of five hundred. Fifty years ago I had caught four hundred lobsters in one week. I put them in the car and left them believing that they would be all right. Lightning struck the car and killed over eighty of them.

During my youth, lobsters were very plentiful and reasonably cheap in price. They had to be hard shelled or the buyers would not take them. We used to catch the largest lobsters then. They were from seven to eight pounds. An old man told me that at one time when they wanted lobsters, his father would go down to the old Spring Market in Portsmouth and get a lobster for thirty cents that would make a chowder for ten in the family.

At that time they did not know what a lobster pot was. Lobsters were caught by means of hoop nets which were large hoops four feet across, made with twine in the form of a checkerboard to hold the lobster. Bait would be tied on the hoop net. The men would have to have about a dozen of these nets. They would have to go back to each one in the night and haul them in. A small piece of wood would be attached to each net and floated on top of the water so they would know where the net was. You had to be pretty clever and quiet in starting those nets from the bottom because a lobster is very quick and if you should disturb him and are not quick enough at starting, off the lobster goes. It took two men to handle the hoop nets, one to row and steady the boat and the other to haul the net. They would catch only one or two lobsters to a net and would bring in on the average of fifty lobsters whereas today with the lobster pots they would in the same amount of time catch two hundred of them. I have seen as high as forty-five lobsters in a trap, a trap not all saleable and some small while the other lobsters were large. I have caught in one week with thirty-five traps, four hundred and eighty in number that would range from one and a half pounds to ten pounds. I have also seen twelve lobsters that would weigh forty pounds in a pot.

On March 15, 1935, while I was hauling in my lobster pots I fell into the ocean and but, for the quick thinking of my grandson, Victor, the fish of the ocean would have eaten me. I was in the process of anchoring the boat when I lost my balance and fell in. If the boat had been moving I would have been drowned as he would not have been able to pull me out in time. A moment of danger that seemed temporarily to place me on the edge of eternity.

Lobstering proved to be my specialty in my work as a fisherman. Why I chose this rather than any other kind I don't know. The lure of the lobster has always had magical effect upon me, and no matter how far away I may be at lobster time, I feel that magic lyre playing its song, enticing me to go to work again.

CHAPTER XIV

NO OTHER trade is more noted for its fabrication of the imagination than that of fishing. To all those who like to delve into humorous conversations, the size of the fish or the intricate method in which it was caught changes its dimensions in a queer Baron Munchausen manner until it bursts through its incredibility. Fishing has been the bunt of these gross exaggerations because for the main part fishing and life upon the treacherous waters abounds with strange tales of monstrous happenings and hideous beings. Men become mere instinctive individuals swayed by the whims of the waves and awed by the tricks that Nature is able to play upon them. No wonder then that tales have drifted from time to time within my life's experiences. The Isles of Shoals has been the center theater for much of this circulating driftwood, many of which has been gathered and regathered until much of the appeal has been lost. I am going to mention some of this driftwood as it has drifted into my mind—a few boards among the many.

One of the most famous stories that has been handed down from one generation of Shoalers to another is that of the Haleys who at one time was a prominent family on Smutty Nose, and whose descendants are at the present time living in Portsmouth. Captain Haley was a sturdy, intelligent Shoaler who lived on the Shoals way back in the early nineteenth century. Once while clambering over the rocks he happened to overturn a slab of stone which was lying face downwards in a conspicuous position. To his surprise he found beneath several bars of solid silver. With wild cries of delight he notified the others and upon reaching the mainland to ascertain their value in coinage, he found them to be worth more than he expected. Presumably, they had been hidden upon the Island by some pirate and his crew, possibly the famous Blackbeard who landed many times in the vicinity of the Islands, and who left in their wake to guard over their treasure, a ghost of a lady and upon foggy nights she may be seen floating about over the rocks. Elated with the large sum of money Captain Haley immediately set to work and built a long-dreamed-of breakwater connecting the island of Smutty Nose with that of Malaga and at the same time insuring a safer locked harbor for the mooring of the boats which were anchored off shore. He also had his own mill with its windmill to grind his corn and he began many improvements in the conditions at Smutty Nose. It is he also who is credited with having had continually a light burning in his window which faced the open sea so that any shipwrecked vessel or any lost driven seacraft would be directed to his shores and thereby saved. Early in the nineteenth century the Spanish ship "Sagunto" was wrecked upon his very shores. As it was cold, biting weather, Captain Haley had gone to bed with no idea of what he was to find in the morning. When he stepped out into his immediate yard the following morning, he found the frozen bodies of three men who had tried to reach the source of the light that beckoned so kindly to them in the bitter pitch blackness and who had failed because the elements had finally overcome them with the agonizing stiffness of the freezing cold about their dripping bodies. Later the bodies of the other members of the shipwrecked crew were found strewn along the coast. The bodies which had been swept up on the shores of the Isles of Shoals were buried with due respect and their graves marked with rough hewn headstones. Out of the wood that drifted in from the ship, Captain Haley built the

old Haley's tavern. He was a great man in many ways as
the epitaph upon his grave denotes:

"In Memory of Mr. Samuel Haley
Who Died In The Year 1811
Aged 84
He Was A Man Of Great Ingenuity
Industry, Honor and Honesty, True To His
Country & A Man Who Did A Great
Publik Good In Building A
Dock & Receiving Into His
Enclosure Many A Poor
Distressed Seaman & Fisherman
In Distress of Weather"

During an Indian massacre on Star Island when all of the
people of the tiny settlement were being butchered one by one,
a woman murdered her two children. Evidently, she had
foreseen the massacre and had time to escape into a small
cavern where she hid with her two tiny children. The children, becoming frightened with the uproar of Indian yelling
and jubilation, cried out. The woman to stifle their cries and
to prevent the Indians from discovering them and mutilating
them, quickly killed the children and thereby indirectly saved
herself.

Miss Underhill's chair is another interesting story of Star.
Miss Underhill was a school teacher who liked to roam about
by herself and to read at her leisure. She had a favorite spot,
a natural carven chair perched upon the rocks overlooking the
rocks where she often went to read. This chair was reasonably above water when the tide was average or low but when
the waves were riding in high it was a dangerous spot for
they would wash right up over the rocks. One day while sitting there and being absorbed in her book, Miss Underhill was

unawaringly swept away by a sudden huge wave and was never heard of again. Since then this place has been known as Miss Underhill's chair. This was on September 11, 1848, and many since this time have sat there but they have always carefully watched the rise of the waves.

In the year 1889, on July the fifteenth, while going out to the fishing grounds, I saved Ben Cobb, one of the six men who was on the sloop "Marion," that started from South Boston for a pleasure cruise along the Rye coast. Out of the six men who set out only one survived and that was Ben Cobb. They set out from South Boston the day before in the pleasure yacht and in the blackness of the night they ran ashore on the rocks. They all rushed for the life boat which was twelve feet in length. However, they did not stay in that long for it was so small in comparison with their number, that it filled with water and four were overturned and drowned. The other two held on to the overturned boat in a desperate try for life. After six hours of fighting to hang on in the cutting water, one of the men by the name of Blackburn slid off from fatigue and went under forever. This was just a short time before I arrived. It was about three o'clock in the morning when I spied the boat filled with water with Ben Cobb holding on for dear life. I sailed to him and took him aboard. He was very fortunate that I had happened to be sailing a certain way, and that he was ahead of my boat in front of my light as it was before daylight and I may have run over him. I was startled at first upon seeing the form of a man in the water, but I soon came to and yelled for him to hold on. My father had always told me that, "a man who had been in the water for a long time would give up quickly if help came." This is just what Cobb did. He let go of his hold and slid back into the water. I grabbed him as quickly as I was able and hauled him aboard with all of my strength. In another five minutes he would have gone under and disappeared from my sight, which was already dimmed by the rising foggy vapor of the early dawn. He lay unconscious in the boat and every once in a while I felt of him to see if he were still breathing. It was a very long way back home. There was very little wind to help me along and as I was unable to do anything medically for the man lying at my feet, I felt that feeling of despair and of slow dragging time. Frantically I rowed to help the sail go faster. And slowly by infinite degrees I managed somehow to reach shore and home port, a distance of over six miles.

Three days before this happened, my baby had been born and on the day on which I brought in Mr. Cobb, my wife was still very ill and weak. As we were coming up toward the house, she heard the noise and commotion of the people about me as I was bringing up the body. She thought that it was I who had been drowned and that they were bringing my body home, she suddenly got out of the bed which proved to be a shock to her in her condition. I could not carry him into my house under these circumstances so my father's house being nearby, I carried him in there and put him to bed. He was a rugged fellow. He had been in the water for an unusually long time. He had been in it so long that the water ran from him out over the bed. However, the doctor said that he would be all right. And so he was.

We notified his brother, who came to take him home. He was from Jamaica Plains, Boston, Mass. I never heard what happened to him after that. He never wrote to me. I never knew who his father was or under what circumstances he lived. When he went out of my father's door it was the last time that I saw or heard of him.

Recent stories of the Isles are beginning to happen. During the last week of July in 1939, there was a fervor of excitement and the waters were thronged with visitors to view the spectacular rescue of the submarine "Squalus." This U. S. submarine "Squalus" was one of the newest of Uncle Sam's submarines being named in honor of the dogfish which "dives fast and swims deep." It cost five million dollars to be built. At seven-thirty on this particular morning she put out from the Portsmouth Navy Yard to practise a fast dive. She carried fifty-one enlisted men, three civilian observers, four officers, and a commander. Two weeks before this time the submarine in being tested had been kept under water for an hour because of a fouled blowout valve. At eight-forty she was off the Isles of Shoals at about five miles when she began to dive. "At the depth gauge of fifty feet she began to level off." Water began pouring into the engine room, the lights became all green on the control board showing that the air valves were shut but with a few exceptions. Between the control and battery rooms there was a bulkhead door where Mate Lyod Maness, an electrician, stood and tugged at the heavy door in order to close it for the ship was at an angle and the door would have to be swung uphill. He had it almost closed when the men, who were beginning to understand that water was to flood them out of the room and life, roared and pleaded to him to keep the door open. He let five of the men through and as the water began to gush against the door, he slammed it tight and clamped down the watertight screw. With this lock, he closed the lives of twenty-six men in the compartment which was rapidly becoming flooded. The commander then sent out smoke bombs to ignite the surface and to show the location of the spot to any ships that might be passing overhead. He also released the deck buoy containing the telephone, which floated to the top of the water and would allow communication to be carried on between those above and those unfortunates below. These men suffered agony from the cold, the dampness and the water pressure which would soon suck up the air in the ship which was only enough to last about eight hours.

A few years ago an officer by the name of Allen R. McCann had been figuring out some way of getting men up from beneath the surface when they were submerged in a submarine. The results of his study and inventive mind was the invention of a bell-shaped chamber which could be lowered from the surface of the water and clamped water tight to the hatch of a submarine. This device would enable the men within to climb into the bell and be lifted up out of the water into safety. Several of these were constructed and at the time of the "Squalus" submersion, the rescue ship "Falcon" steamed up from New London with the bell. First a diver went under and was lowered to the deck of the "Squalus" where he slid a shackle over a ring on the submarine's deck, clipped a bolt through and tightened the nut, in this way establishing a heavy cable line up to the "Falcon." The rescue bell reeled on this line, and the bell was clamped over the hatch and seven men climbed into the bell. On the second day of the sinking the men, but for the unfortunate twenty-six, had been rescued safely.

I am very well acquainted with the grounds in which the "Squalus" sunk. All my fishing days I have caught fish in the place where she made her last dive. It is on the same bottom that we used to catch the large codfish in the winters of the eighties. We used to call it the Hole. It is about the deepest water in Ipswich Bay near the Isles of Shoals. I realized how hard they had to work to get the submarine into more shallow water for I know the ground as well as my own floor, having sailed over it so often. It was a magnificent piece of rescue work and will be remembered throughout all history. I know because I watched it and I know the might of the old ocean. During the first night of the sinking, some reporters came down from Boston for me to take them out in the middle of the night. They said they would give me a hundred dollars to take them. It was a bad night to be out on the sea and thunderstorms were about and it was as black as pitch dungeon. I had the new boat so I decided not to take any chances of going out eighteen miles to sea. My father once told me, "John, on the ocean think of your safety first." And throughout my many ventures out upon the deep this thought has come first to my mind. Although I was never exactly afraid of the old ocean, I always tried to apply good common sense. They were disappointed at my refusal and went off. The next morning I carried four men out to take pictures for the Pathe Weekly. They were able to take some fine pictures. We arrived at the scene just as the first bell came up with seven men. It was some sight just to see the expression on these poor men's faces as they were being brought back to life.

Another recent murder which has centered about the Isles of Shoals is the recent slaying which took place on July 1940. It resembles the Smutty Nose Murder in the fact that there was an argument over the Maine or New Hampshire jurisdiction of the case.

A twenty-two year old boy, John Field, Jr., of Monhegan Island, Maine, murdered a Stanley Wakem on the seiner "Njorth." He had attended Portland High School and while there had attained an average rating while having participated in sports and while being very popular among the boys. He left school in his Junior year and his family moved to Port Clyde, Maine. The boy in his early teens portrayed an unusual marked mania for religious worship. He worked on fishing boats and his last job had been this crew work with the "Njorth." It seems that Fields struck Wakem with a four foot iron pump handle and fractured his skull for no reason being given whatsoever. The slaying took place in the old Gosport Harbor in the schooner lying off the Isles of Shoals.

Since New Hampshire has capital punishment and Maine does not, it was a serious matter in the trial as to where the case was to be tried. The Federal Government had no claim to decide the issue since it was within the twelve mile limit and in the territory of the two towns. As better facilities were provided at York, Maine, the boy was taken to York, as was Louis Wagner. While he was in jail he kept reading and being absorbed in his Bible and sat always calmly displaying a blank innocence. He was tried and convicted of third degree murder and got a life sentence in Maine.

Such is some of the driftwood that has been washed in upon my sands of time. Rumors of the tragedies of man's mishaps in the face of Nature and machine, played upon the waters as a stage and before the audience of law and curiosity, in a theatre of universal custom. Driftwood that never fails to drift upon each generation of mankind.

CHAPTER XV

THE PISCATAQUA is one of the most interesting rivers of New Hampshire. Flowing from the north to the south, winding its way through until it reaches its mouth when it blends with the Atlantic Ocean, this river has proven its worth by the courageous and industrious deeds performed by those peoples who have from time to time lived along its shores. All of my life I have been up and down this river; from one end to the other. It is one of the most delightful spots for recreation and business. It never freezes in the winter no matter how cold, and its tides ebb and flow at about eight miles an hour, allowing those who wish to play or work a comfortable journey.

The Piscataqua is in no small way responsible for the growth and historical development of the City of Portsmouth; being an inlet from the sea and lending safety in its rock bottomed harbor from encroaching storms and enemies. The harbor in itself is a landlocked harbor with plenty of water deep enough for any ship of any make to enter in any kind of weather. I have seen this harbor a few years ago just filled with all types of vessels from one mast to seven masts. In those days it was about all sailing vessels coal-laden, for this port is one of the largest ports in New England. When other harbors froze up along the Atlantic Coast, this harbor was clear. Vessels and ships can come and go at any time. New Castle was at the mouth of the harbor. They would send about thirty vessels to the Banks in the spring. This was at the time of the big saltfishing. Jerry, a man by the name of Donne, had ten of the largest fishing vessels. That was back in the seventies. The fish were plentiful and not far away. The vessels would come home loaded down with salt fish of every kind but now the fishing is passing away along the shore line of the old Piscataqua. You have to go way out into deep water to catch any. I don't know why in those gone by days the fish used to go inshore to spawn and breed but now you can't catch even one.

The name of Piscataqua comes from the Indian language. As John Smith toured along the coast line he gave to this part of the country the name of "Passataquack." It is historically mentioned as having been derived from the roots of the Abenaki. The Abenaki were a race of Indians who occupied the country between the Penobscot River and the territory near the Piscataqua. It is reported that an Indian translated it for Mr. Jenness as meaning, "the place where three rivers make one." Like so many of the other rivers which cut through New England, it has retained the Indian language which abounded along its shores in pre-colonial days.

Indian folklore, struggles between the early Indian tribes and the early colonists for the right of domination, exists today along the Piscataqua. One of the best known is that of the governing influences of Major Richard Waldron who in 1676 signed a peace treaty with the Indians, the Piscataqua and Cascos. During the time of King Phillip's war several of the Indians, who had participated in war dances and raids, were placed in the Dover jail for safe keeping. These Indians becoming bold and fearless escaped from the meager jail and running about the Indians' camps in the surrounding forests, incited them to action against the whites. Some of the Indians from the Southern woods were friendly with Major Waldron, living in the same neighborhood with their squaws and children. Not knowing just what strategy to pursue to save the lives of the whites about him, Waldron and the other men decided to take the Indians prisoners before they had time to join as allies with the warlike Indians. Waldron invited the Indians to a sham fight and during it he surrounded the Indians with real arms and ammunitions and disarmed them entirely. The Pennacooks were set free, the rest, about two hundred or more, were sent back to Boston as prisoners, among them being "one-eyed John and Sagamore Sam." Six or seven were tried and hanged for past offences, while many of the others were sold into slavery.

From then on, Waldron was hated by the Pennacook and surrounding Indian tribes for his treachery to their friends. In 1677 he had more trouble with the Indians. The laws regarding the rights of the Indian tribes having become more strict with the passing years: "all Indians should be settled at Quochecho, no Indians had the right to travel in the woods this side of the Merrimac without the permit of Major Waldron." Then came a series of murders of the white men which happened under cover of the dense woods and several houses were burned to the ground. All the surrounding communities rushed to their garrisons for protection. Waldron went eastward to try to stop these actions but he was unable to do so. Later on, peaceful agreements were proposed and peace having been declared with the chiefs by a tribute of corn being promised, these skirmishes ended for the time being.

King William's War in 1689 woke up the Indians to more trouble and the settlers again were doubly suspicious of undermining Indian subversive activities but Major Waldron reassured them by saying: "Go plant your pumpkins." An Indian chief named Mesandowit supped at Waldron's house and said, "Suppose strange Indians come now, Brother Waldron." Waldron retorted: "I have but to raise my finger and one hundred soldiers will be at my command." That same evening Waldron let two squaws sleep on the hearth by the kitchen fire. As Waldron was barring the door for the night, one of the squaws said: "White father, big wampum, much Indian come." Just before dawn they came. The squaws rose and opened the doors. The Indians swarmed into Waldron's room. He sprang from his bed, and although over eighty years of age held them back with his sword, but was at last felled, killed and butchered. His house was burned, his daughter and grandchild taken captive, his son-in-law killed. This was the famous massacre along the old Piscataqua where the early colonists fared through difficult and trying times to be able to build a promising city in later years through their foundation of courage and daring and sacrifice.

The scenery along the Piscataqua changes from year to year with the improvements of its banks and the alterations in its bridges yet the best description that I have ever read and the most touching is that of C. S. Gueney in his book, "Portsmouth Historic And Picturesque."

"The Piscataqua River, to which Portsmouth owes so much, and to which in the future it must necessarily be indebted, as well as the State of New Hampshire, for the existence of its only seaport, is properly not a river at all, but a long, narrow, crooked and deep-channeled arm of the sea, extending into the land in a westerly direction about a dozen miles making three rectangular turns on the way, and then expanding into the broad sheet of water called the Great Bay. A number of small rivers, of which the principal are the Cocheco and the Salmon Falls, flow into it, but these, even during the period of their spring freshets, have no perceptible effect on the height of the tides of the Piscataqua, the current of which is so swift, owing to the peculiar formation of the inlet and the filling and emptying of Great Bay at every tide, that the harbor never freezes over.

"A row or sail on the Piscataqua, in either direction from the City, is a thoroughly enjoyable experience to any one with even a moderate appreciation of Nature's attractions; but it should never be undertaken by a person unacquainted with the river, unaccompanied by a local river-man. But an imaginary trip on the Piscataqua is perfectly safe; let us take one. Looking northerly up the river from Portsmouth Bridge with Kittery on the right hand and Freeman's Point on the left, a half mile or so distant appears the village of Eliot Neck. Here the river makes a turn to the westward at a right angle. Freeman's point, formerly one of the most beautiful spots in this picturesque section of the country, is now the scene of great industrial activity, many hundreds of men with horses and much machinery being engaged in leveling hills, filling valleys and otherwise altering the face of Nature, preparatory to the erection of what is to be the largest paper-mill in the world. The Kittery shore of the river, above the bridge, is still as beautiful as ever.

"Below the bridge, on the river front, are many points of historic interest, of which only the briefest mention can be made. First on the westerly, or New Hampshire, side is Nobel's Island, formerly a noted fishing station and later the building place of many ships, and is now owned by the Boston & Maine Railroad. Just below the Island are the railroad coal wharves of J. A. & A. W. Walker which included the site of what was once Rindge's Wharf, where the frigate 'Raleigh' later run ashore on the coast of Maine and captured by a British squadron after a hard fight, was built for the Continental Navy in 1776; and where the sloop-of-war 'Ranger,' the first warship to display the stars and stripes as the American ensign and in which John Paul Jones went to England in 1777 capturing the British sloop-of-war 'Drake' on the way, was built after the 'Raleigh' was launched, and on the same blocks.

Where once floated the 'Raleigh' and the 'Ranger' can now be seen coal schooners several times larger than both of them together, and steam diggers lifting out several tons of coal a minute. Next below is Gray & Prime's coal wharf, where the late Edward F. Sise started the 'sea coal' business in Portsmouth; the Isles of Shoals steamboat and other wharves; and where the river makes one of its right angles is the ferry station of the Portsmouth, Kittery & York Street Railway, formerly the Spring Market. From the ferry house to Church Point are lofty brick warehouses, five stories high on the river front and two or three stories high on the street, reminders of the times when Portsmouth's foreign trade was very great; and towering above them is old St. John's Church, on the apex of Church Hill. Passing around Church Point—an easy thing to do if the tide is running that way, but not otherwise—the Portsmouth Brewing Company, the new power house of the Rockingham County Light and Power Company, the navy landing, lumber wharves and another coal wharf, and then next you observe the new, commodious house of the Portsmouth Yacht Club and Peirce's Island, which forms one side of the Narrows. On the Maine side of the river, just below the bridge, are fields and farms of Kittery, the old Rice house, close to which was the old time ferry landing, Badger's Island and the navy yard. Badger's Island, now the Kittery landing of the Portsmouth, Kittery & York Railway Ferry, was for many years a noted shipyard, more than a hundred vessels, many of them of large size, having been built there, among them the 'America,' the first 74-gun ship ever built on this side of the Atlantic, the construction of which, on blocks but a few rods from the present ferry landing, was superintended by John Paul Jones, and which was launched under his personal direction and command. Of the navy yard no further mention need be made here.

"Passing through the Narrows, on the right is seen, at the top of the steep bank of Peirce's Island, old Fort Washington, and an extensive earthwork built in 1775, and strongly armed and garrisoned during the Revolution under the command of Captain Titus Salter, and again armed and equipped in 1812-15. Next on the same side is Shapley's Island, separated from Peirce's only by a boat channel, and not even by that at low tide; this island was once a noted shipyard. Here the main river makes a turn to the left at a right angle, but the Little Harbor Branch keeps straight on to the southward, broadening out near the sea into Little Harbor, now improved by dredging and breakwaters into an excellent harbor of refuge for small vessels. This branch is spanned, between Shapeley's and Goat Islands, by a drawbridge; and Goat Island and Great Island—the latter being the town of New Castle— are connected by a road recently built on top of the government breakwater, beside the old pile bridge. From Goat Island to Fort Point, along the main river, the New Castle shore is occupied by quaint old houses and new summer cottages, and at Fort Point the river takes another turn at a right angle, and goes straight out to sea in a southerly direction. At Fort Point is old Fort Constitution, formerly Fort William and Mary, and outside of the old fortification is the wreck of the new Fort Constitution, commenced at the close of the Civil War, and planned to be a granite fortress with three tiers of guns, but the work was abandoned after many thousand dollars had been spent thereon. There is now a new battery there of modern guns, near the old breastworks, and another fort is being built at Jaffrey's Point, the southern extremity of the island. At Fort Constitution is also a lighthouse, officially known as Portsmouth Harbor Light, on the site of a former wooden tower one hundred and fifteen feet high, built before the Revolution, during the administration of Governor John Wentworth.

"Returning to the Narrows, on the left is Henderson's Point, the southwesterly point of Seavey's Island, which is now a part of the navy yard. The government at the present time have a large force at work removing this obstruction to navigation, to the depth of thirty-five feet, allowing vessels of the greatest draught to pass over what is now, but soon to be no more, Henderson's Point. Here are range lights for the guidance of mariners coming up river at night, and a house for the light-keeper; not far away is a pretty little house known as the Greely cottage, in which General Greely, now of the national signal service, rested for several weeks after his fearful experience in the Arctic regions. Just to the eastward of the Greely cottage, at the top of the highest point of Seavey's Island, seventy feet above the water, is a curving rampart of stone, looking something like a fort. It is not a fort, however, but the top of an open reservoir made by digging out old Fort Sullivan and cementing the inside of the hole. Fort Sullivan was built in 1775 and was armed and garrisoned in 1812 and again during the Civil War. Just back of it is the tall stand-pipe of the navy yard water system. At the easterly end of the island is the slope where the Spanish War prisoners were confined. A little farther down the river is Clark's Island, treeless and uninhabited, with Jamaica Island, the summer home of a wealthy gentleman, back of it and near the Kittery shore. Then the channel down on the charts as Crooked Lane, and then Kittery Point, with its ancient church, its summer hotels and cottages and its many pretty homesteads, and old Fort McClary, once of much importance as a harbor fortification but now useless, though guns were mounted there during the war with Spain. At Kittery Point Village are the former homes of the Brays, Pepperells and Sparhawks, and the anchorage between the village beach and the Fishing Islands is called Pepperell's Cove. From Kittery Point to the ocean front extends Gerrish Island, which to the passerby appears to be a part of the mainland, and which is largely taken up by the summer homes of wealthy people, though not far from the sea is Fort Foster, a strong fortification recently built, and right on the sea front is a summer hotel and a number of cottages. There are several small islands at the mouth of the harbor, including Wood Island, which has no wood on it; and marking the entrance is Whaleback Lighthouse, a tall granite structure with an iron tower containing a fog signal apparatus in its rear. The outer island of all is a mere ledge of rocks, is White Island. From Portsmouth Bridge to the ocean, almost every spot along the banks of the river is of historic or traditional interest."

When the excursion was made in this imaginary manner life along the banks was much duller than it is today. Defense orders are causing the City to boom with bustle and commotion as well as vast improvements along the shore lines. Selectees swarm the islands about Kittery and anti-aircraft guns guard every right angle of the river, while each day new submarines may be seen docked outside the navy yard. There, too, is a brand new bridge that spans the Piscataqua.

In 1794 Portsmouth was connected with Dover Point by a bridge over the Piscataqua flowing into the Great Bay. This bridge which was build by the formation of a corporation was two thousand three hundred and sixty-two feet long and thirty-eight feet wide. Tolls were collected and soon as the years passed the amount proved to be inadequate for the expense of the repairs so that in May, 1804, a "Piscataqua Bridge Lottery" was carried out under the sponsorship of the "New Hampshire Gazette," to supply the money for another new bridge and in May 1805 the new bridge was opened to the traffic.

Previously to 1923 the old route into Maine was over the old

Portsmouth to Kittery toll bridge which was operated by the Boston and Maine railroad which directed the traffic through the business section down Market Street across Noble's Island and the toll bridge. The Memorial Bridge was the first steel structure to span the Piscataqua. This bridge was opened for traffic seventeen years ago August 23, 1923. My brother Edward was alderman at this time and my brother Alexander fractured his leg twice while working on it.

Two sterling silver shears gleamed out on November 8, 1940, when two seven-year old girls opened the new three million dollar interstate bridge to motorists. All during 1939-1940 men had been toiling in the wake of gale, ice and sun to build this magnificent superstructure which overtowers the old Piscataqua which has so often withstood changes of nature and man. Trains will run on the lower deck and motor traffic will be overhead; the towers are more than two hundred feet high. Like a mighty arm of protection it wings its way over connecting the two states of Maine and New Hampshire.

From one bridge to another, from the old to the new, from the newly wrought to the newly improved, ever and ever better and larger the waters of the Piscataqua are being spanned. Airplanes overhead, motor cars and pedestrians crossing over and to recross again. How many times have I motored over and motored under this bridge while watching and thinking of the long procession of traffic flowing along and seeing the rich, the middle, and the poor stream pass, many of them entering and many of them going out of life's doors. How much of the mysteries of life has this river witnessed in its course. Life passing over it, life passing on it, and life going on with it, and minute phrases of life being wormed out beneath it. How much happiness has it brought to those who swim in it and to those who merrily sail with the winds over it. And how much tragedy and sorrow has it caused to the many who through shipwreck, drowning or neglect have been upset into it. And how much throughout my life's career have I depended on this mighty river for my protection against the flux of living.

CHAPTER XVI

CLAMS

UP FROM the mud and the sand come the signs of the clam. Little air holes dot the beaches and shores when the tide is out. Every fisherman at some time has gone home with an aching back from digging the clams out of these tell-tale signs. The digging of clams is a tedious and dirty business, but there is never a time when the tide runs out that you will not see a man rowing his rowboat out to get them; or else you see him coming home with his basket full. My back has ached from having dug too many clams a little too anxiously about the beaches and river beds and I have brought back baskets full in my earlier life.

New England is mighty proud of her clams. Wherever you go, you find that the names of the Seabrook and Ipswich clam are well known and famous as well as being well liked as a food. A clam was called a clam way back in the old days by the early colonists from the tight manner in the way the clam clamped or closed its shell when it was in danger. The Indians used to call them "quohogs." These Indians were accustomed to dig them, salt and sell them to the early fishermen as bait for cod fish. William Wood says of the early New England clams:

"Clamms or clamps is a shel-fish not much unlike a cockle, it lyeth under the sand every six or seaven of them having a round hole to take ayre and receive water at. When the tide ebs and flowes, a man running over these clam banks will presently be made all wet by their spouting of water out of those small holes;—In some places of the country there bee Clamms as big as a pennie white loafe, which are great dainties amongst the natives and would bee in good esteeme amongst the English were it not for better fish."

The Indians used the shells of the clams as their wampum money, after they had dug out the meat and eaten it. I remember that even the Indians that visited the Shoals had strings of clam shells wound about their necks. They made use of the hard shell clam which is of a brown color. Clams are found in from one to six fathoms of water off the Atlantic Coast from Florida to Cape Cod and are also found in large quantities off New Brunswick. The large clam, or giant clam as it is called, is from five to seven inches long. It is white within and without when dead and worn by the effects of heavy weather. Alive it has a skin of pale brown. It lives close to the water mark and so near to the surface that it is easily dug out with a short stick or even with the fingers.

My father used to store chopped clams on board ship whenever we went out on a trip for mackerel. He would use these for jig line fishing up the mackerel. The chopped clams were used for bait and lowered down into the water alongside to entice the mackerel to come around the boat. The crew enjoyed jigging up the mackerel as it was great fun watching the squirming fish try to let go the hook.

Mackerel like the salted clams but the codfish delighted in eating them. They would eat the whole clam shell and all on the ocean bottom, spitting out the shells as they ate out the meat. The "bank clam" was what they hunted for the most. The "bank clam" is a fairly large clam with a brownish blue-black discolored shell. They are generally found on the ocean bottom. Cod like them, and around the clam banks you were always sure to get a large catch. Clams must have been plentiful in early times because there were so many codfishing vessels about. It is said that "in the codfishery alone Massachusetts had 4,000 men and 28,000 tons of shipping before the Revolutionary War, the fleet being largely composed of sloops."

We caught our largest hauls of codfish off Ipswich Bay and one of the reasons for that was the fact that about Ipswich Bay there were many clams. Herring was our chief bait but salted clams were used more than once. The men would dig the clams, bring them to the Shoals, and the women would pick out the meats and place them in large barrels of salt which we placed on our vessels. All the large sailing vessels in the early days used the clam as bait. One story that I read by Wesley George Pierce told me this:

"We stowed 60 barrels of shucked and salted clams for fish bait. William T. Maddocks, who owned fine 'Bankers' in the eighties, bought the bait (salted clams) for his vessels in Portland. The five vessels required about 250 barrels and the price paid was $5.50 per barrel. The 'clammers' were men who lived around Harpswell Bay and they sold their clams to Portland dealers. These clammers had to dig their bait for the most part in March, for during January and February the flats were often covered with ice. The men were able by hard work to dig several bushels (in the shell) each low tide (two a day) as the clams were very plentiful in that locality. It was a smart man who could dig enough clams in one day to shuck out a barrel of meats. Shucking was done at high water, and also during the evening. About all the Down East vessels bought their bait in Portland, the industry giving employment to several hundred men, for there must have been about a hundred sail of vessels requiring an average of fifty barrels each or a total of 5000 barrels."

An amateur clam digger has some difficulty in digging out clams whole. He finds the hole, digs in with his stick, and while taking out the clam he inevitably breaks its shell. An expert clam digger takes the clam right out whole with little trouble. He throws them one after the other into his hollow basket which he always carries with him. He then takes the clams in the basket and systematically runs the basket up and down in the water to wash the mud or sand off the clams.

Professional clam diggers lived on Rings Island in Newburyport, Mass., on the Merrimac. There are large clam flats there. The clam diggers live in little huts along the shore. These people are a hard working class in their own way. Years ago there would be piles and piles of clam shells lying in back of these huts like pavements when the diggers were so busy that they did not have time to clean up the shells and just had to let them stay there.

Clam digging is a business by itself. You cannot find clams everywhere. Yet, in certain spots men do nothing else to make a living. Hampton River is the only place in New Hampshire where they make a real business of it. On the Seabrook side at Seabrook beach there are about fifty men who make their living on clams and lobsters. It is an old beach, dating way back into colonial history, and many of the early fishermen, as well as Indians, are said to have clammed there. Men were born and grew up with the clams from boyhood in the steps of their fathers. The tide there goes out for miles and miles and leaves the flats all day. The quantity of clams dug there is large and they are distributed and sold all over.

Of late the law in New Hampshire requires that a business man pay a fee to dig clams to carry on his work and an amateur pays fifteen cents if he wants to dig up enough for his dinner. Sometimes you almost break your back in order to get enough for dinner. As in all kinds of work, the men who earn their bread and butter by it, know just where to dig in order to make their profits. There is one head man

who buys up all the clams the clam diggers have to sell. He
hires help. Women open the clams for market and he sends
them on to markets elsewhere.

This year the market sales have fallen. People are not
traveling as much. You can always find a market for clams.
People love to come out themselves to dig. They use a forked
stick in the same manner as is used for digging potatoes.

Clams are a delicious sea food and served with melted
butter are appetizing. Clams, before they are sold to a
customer, have to be opened and thoroughly washed and put
into cans to go to the market. From the markets they are
sold principally to restaurants and to parties for clam bakes.
Clam bakes are famous along New England coasts. Baking
the clams by means of hot stones is a popular sport especially
at Fourth of July.

That's what the Old Sea always gives us—something in
return for our work. She builds up our inwards with the
vitamins and calories necessary for our muscles and bones
with the food she harbors in her deep. Her sea weed, green
and slimy, shelters the large clams in her folds to provide
food for man. I have been on the sea for seventy years and
always I wonder at each new creature that is turned up, caught
and cleaned to give us life. The ranchmen have their cattle
to carry to market, the farmer has his chickens, and the
fisherman has his fish to carry. No truer words are written
than those of Whittier in his poem on "The Fishermen:"

> "From our fish, as in the old time,
>   The silver coin shall come.
> As the demon fled the chamber
>   Where the fish of Tobit lay,
> So ours from all our dwellings
>   Shall frighten Want away."

CHAPTER XVII

QUEEN OF THE OCEAN

SITTING alone upon the Isles and looking out over the water, I watched day after day as I was growing up, the numerous white sails that floated in and out, around and about, touching up the blue-green of the ocean with their colorful hulls of all sizes. I hung about the wharf while their cargoes were unloaded, and watched the crew jerk up and down the ropes, astonished at their skill and agility. As I grew a little older and helped my father in his work, I began to learn what these vessels were made of, and to realize that to manipulate a sailing ship is an art rather than a trade.

A fisherman or a seaman is not one unless he can have his hand trained in the art of carving out and fashioning a boat. The crew members from the boys up to the captain of the old fishing fleets had to be ready at any time to help patch up a hole caused by some freak incident. More than once I have helped to pitch in either to seal up a hole or to mend a partly split canvas. Few men there were who did not have in those days a shelter or spare space for boat building and mending. My grandfather had a special second story to his barn where he fashioned out his boats during the winter.

The first kind of sail boat to sail in and out of the Shoals was what they used to call the "Gundalow." The "Gundalow" was a flat-bottomed boat with a "shortmast" and "leg o'mutton" sail. She sailed up and down the Piscataqua and was used as a cargo ship to carry goods up and down, from one colony to another in 1650, along the New England sea coast. It is written that "when Fort William and Mary was captured from the British by patriots on the night of December 14, 1776, powder that was used in this attack was carried up the river in the 'Gundalow.'" Many of these early colonists were saved from starvation and complete isolation by these slow moving boats.

This "Gundalow" changed form many times and its hull became more trimmed and hollowed out and the sails caught the wind more gracefully until the colonies grew in population, extent, and needs. Wooden ship construction increased in output. Designs became larger and more elaborate until the clipper ship was evolved. These were the large ships that sailed in and out and they were in demand, for they were what the traders wanted—beauty and speed. Then came the big gold rush in California of 1849 when swarms of men enticed by the promise of wealth set out in anything they could get hold of. The large shipping concerns of Eastport, Portland, and Boston saw a good chance to make a good sum of money with exceptional profit and so they set right to it. They saw that it was much faster to sail around from the East, around the tip of South America to reach San Francisco, than it was to cover the territory through Indian covered fields and mountains, so they built the big clippers to carry many passengers. Not only were the vast tracts of land covered with the white hoods of the covered wagon, but the two oceans were dotted with white wings of the ships driving through the ocean to catch the sight of glittering gold.

Early seamen called this sail boat "Queen of the Ocean." The first ship to be rightly named a clipper was the "Ann McKim" in 1832. She had very thick set lines and ran heavy in the sea. After her they made the clipper with sharper bow and fancier lines. At first the sails tended to outweigh the hull and it was hard for the ship to withstand heavy gales and the onslaught of dashing waves without causing her to slacken her speed or to heel over. The gold rush proved that this type of ship was worth building and trading posts decided that the unusual speed would save them many a dollar in crossing the Atlantic. They then fashioned them so that they could make the distance to China and Australia in one-half the time. America received from then on the bulk of the European trade. In 1859 the noted clipper "Dreadnought" made the trip across the choppy Atlantic to Europe in twelve days. Donald McKay of Boston, of whom I had heard my grandfather speak so often, was the greatest of all clipper builders, having put many a fast and speedy clipper on her way. He used the best of oak and pine to be found in the New England forests and made his cabins out of mahogany and rosewood. "A great many of these ships were painted black with a gold red stripe about the hull. The clipper, 'Lightning,' which McKay built in 1854, established herself as the fastest sailing vessel in the world by a run of 436 miles in twenty-four hours. This record was unequalled by steamships for many years."

These craft were of every shape and manner and of every shade in the rainbow. The traders from the North, South, East, and West came into the harbor with their vessels made from the produce of their local forests and as they were of every race they brought over the peculiarities of decorations and omens. There were diverse ways of handling the ships that had been passed down from father to son, captain to crew. Brightly colored flags decorated the masts and these fluttered vigorously. From England came the terms for the sails. The sails were supported and held up by means of masts, yards, gaffs, booms, bowsprit spars and staves of slanting ropes. The first sail on the "Gundalow" was a square sail and as the vessels grew bigger and bigger they added on more shapes from quadrangulars to triangulars. There were two sets of these, the square rigged and the fore- and aft-rigged. The mast nearest the bow head is known as the fore-mast, the next abaft or nearest the middle of the ship as the main-mast, and the third or that nearest the stern as the mizzen-mast. Each mast consisted of several sections that were called the lower or standing mast, the next above that the top-mast, the next the top-gallant-mast, above which was the royal-mast. Each of these sails had its respective yard with which it was slung. This was all part of the rigging.

Every man was expected to be thoroughly acquainted with the rigging of the vessel in which he served, and when he had charge of the ship, such as being the Master, he had to frequently examine every part to see that it was efficiently working; he had to see that it was neither too taut nor too slack, nor that it had been worn by wet, chafing or some unexpected injury. Each one was supposed to have a general knowledge of what to do rather than to be a well studied navigator. He was to be able to sew a seam and to assist the sailmaker in the repairing of the sails. Above all, he had to know how to tie knots, bends and splices and when to use them in the parts of the rigging and equipment of a ship. All the heavy weights of the rigging had to be looked after for there could not be too much strain at any one section especially on the ends of the boats. The bows and sterns of schooners and sailing yachts should be empty.

Anchoring one of these sailing ships was a pretty touchy job. She should never lie long at single anchor in a tide-way during the variable winds, for she would be apt to foul her anchor and do away with its hold in the water. If she had more than the one anchor, the one to be weighed was that which it would be the least convenient to sail from. The direction of the tide was always very important. If the anchors dragged and she struck the bottom, especially where there were rocks, she would be apt to scrape her hull and go to pieces in deep water. If this had happened, that she would be dragging anchor, the Captain should have looked for a good place on the shore line, if there were any such spot at the time, and he would have thrown her into it by slipping or breaking all the cables and making sail speedy enough to drive her in with the hopes that she would drive high enough to save the lives on board by landing her, very much in the same manner in which an airplane would make a forced landing.

The Captain had to be ready at any time for an occurrence of the three main possible disasters on these ships — man falling overboard, fire, and collision. He had to have the crews drilled and practiced for any such emergency. At that time when a man was overboard the Captain would order the vessel to be turned about and a boat would be lowered to pick the man up. Every member had to guard against fire by always taking care to prevent one happening. Fire drill was ordinary. At the sound of the alarm all ports and ventilators had to be closed, wind-sails hauled up, hatchways to be closed wherever possible, all the lower sails taken in and the ship kept before the wind unless the fire was in the after part and then it was a matter of lowering and manning the boats immediately. No one could safeguard the ship against the collision with a stationary or moving object. Fogs, gales, reefs, could not be forecast accurately and when the vessel was veering in or about these it was a mad scramble for doing the right thing at the right time if it were possible. It was more or less a matter of luck and daring on the part of the crew and many times much cargo was lost through collision.

The lines of these famous old sailing vessels are still making stirring history today. The noted airline clippers are nothing but the hulls of these boats with wings on of aluminum instead of canvas; cutting through the air instead of water. From Lisbon to New York, from the horrors of war-torn Europe to our shores, people have been flown to their freedom as in the old days they were spared the massacres of the Indians by sailing to their destinations. These planes may be a great deal more speedy and streamlined but they still have only a small measure of the spunk and dash of the old clippers—"Queens of the Ocean."

CHAPTER XVIII

EACH of us at some time in life wonders about the lives and experiences of those who preceded us in the years gone by and who were connected to us by blood relationship. Each of us likes to go back and catch a glimpse into the workings of these long departed relatives who meant so much to the development of their community and their country; who blazed the trails and smoothed the paths for our coming; and who so gallantly waged their battles for their survival in an enemy's wilderness. Whether they be the man behind the hoe, the man behind the wheel or the man who believes in doing nothing at all, they make their mark by which each of us is able to turn back and check upon them. Every mark discovered is worth its weight in gold and leaves us to ponder over it within our memories.

I found that the traces of the marks left by my ancestors had been left about the old "Strawberry Bank." This early "Strawberry Bank" covered the grounds of Portsmouth, Rye, New Castle, Newington, and Greenland. This was in the year of 1635 and before this year a John Berry is said to have become the first settler of Rye at Sandy Beach. He was the son of William Berry who had been sent out by Mason, the founder of New Hampshire, and given a "plantation and who was at Portsmouth as early as 1631." William Berry died before June, 1654. His widow, Jane, married Nathaniel Drake. "January, 1648-49 at a town meeting held at Strawberry Bank," it was "granted that William Berry shall have a lot upon a neck of land upon the South side of the Little River at Sandy Beach."

The early Berry family after having founded and formed a small settlement at Rye, New Hampshire, intermarried frequently with the Locke family who had also settled within this district. Throughout the generations these two families had a strange attraction for one another and scattered in and out the years there were many marriages between them. A Jeremiah Berry born in 1721, married a Hannah Locke, then, at her death, he married one Eleanor Brackett. He was a "corporal in Captain Parsons' Company in the Revolutionary War, and was stationed at New Castle." Patty Berry, who was born July 21, 1792, married March 22, 1809, a Job Foss who was my great grandfather on my Grandmother Down's side.

Land seemed to be of the utmost importance to the Sandy Beach settlers. Sandy Beach or Foss's Beach, as it is sometimes called, was divided and re-divided many times among the original families. Parsons writes that "In 1649, there was granted unto Anthony Brackett a lot between Robert Puddington's and William Berry's, at the head of the Sandy Beach, Fresh River, at the western bank thereof. William Seavey had given him three acres at a town meeting held at Strawberry Bank (Portsmouth in 1652). It is granted by common consent that William Berry shall have a lot upon the neck of land upon the south side of the Little River at Sandy Beach.

"Land was granted by the town of Portsmouth to William Seavey in 1652. Coming by south side of the Mill creek at the head of Hodges' land and run west to 'White Rock' fifty acres the same laid out to his son William Seavey in 1721. At a town meeting held in Portsmouth in 1653 a committee was chosen to lay out the lands unto the people of Sandy Beach, viz.: 'Unto William Berry six acres of meadow unto his house that is by William Seavey's; to Anthony Brackett, thirty acres upland adjoining unto his house and twenty acres of meadow; to Thomas Seavey eight acres of meadow and eight acres of upland for a lot; to James Johnson twenty acres of meadow; between said Creek and the Creek's mouth, and four acres of land where he hath already ploughed.'

"In 1660 land was apportioned at Sandy Beach as follows: 'Anthony Brackett, thirteen acres; James Johnson, and Mr. Wallis, one hundred twelve acres; John Berry, thirteen acres; John Odiorne, forty-three acres; John Foss, nineteen acres; Mr. Mason, thirty-five acres; Frau Rann (Rand), fifty acres, thitry extra; Nathaniel Drake, fifty acres; Anthony Brackett 1st, one hundred acres.'

"In 1723 land was laid out as follows: 'To Joshua Foss, Jacob Clark, Widow Clark together with the share of John Foss, deceased, beginning at stake in road east to Rag hole, 106 rods, to Joseph Locke's corner and then by said Locke's line east, 24 rods, then 26 rods as the road goes to complete that piece; to Samuel Berry, begin at corner of Richard Goss's old grant by the south side of the Rag hole highway. West by said Berry's land 36 rods square up with William Berry's land, to the south end of Goss's old grant then east 30 rods to Rag hole highway and the remainder of Hodge's common right and Robert Jordon's being 18 acres together with the above makes their quantity 25 acres.' "

These exchanges of land grants complicated the matters of Rye but did not cause one-half the trouble that did holding on to the land from the frequent raidings of the Indians and attempting to protect their wives and children from the daring scalping parties that took place along this beach. There are many stories of the daring and suffering of these staunch and stubborn colonists. Records show that they endured much to preserve this land. There is an account by Parsons in his "History of Rye" that explains fully to what extent these raids were carried out.

"Sandy Beach, in common with many others of the early settlements, suffered terribly from Indian raids. Men, women, and children were slaughtered or carried into captivity, houses and barns destroyed by fire, and cattle killed. The settler and his family, when they lay down for the night, had no assurance that they would not be aroused before morning by the warwhoop of the savages, to find their dwellings in flames and all chance of escape cut off. How many of the Sandy Beach pioneers perished through these sudden and deadly attacks is not known, but the number is large. The records of Indian depredations on the settlement are very meagre and incomplete, but the most disastrous raid of which there is authentic record took place in September, 1691, when a party of savages, variously estimated at from twenty to forty, came from the eastward in canoes and landed at Sandy Beach. They did not attack the garrison house there, but killed some of the defenseless families living on or in near vicinity to Brackett's lane (now known as Brackett's road), took a number of persons captive, and burned several small houses. Anthony Brackett, who lived near Saltwater brook, was killed, and was buried on the eastern side of the highway; his will was proved in 1692. Goodman Rand's family also suffered in this raid," concerning which Dow, in his "History of Hampton" says:

"Two messengers brought the sad intelligence to Hampton. On their return in the evening, on reaching Ragged Neck, about half a mile south of the Sandy Beach garrison house, they saw, as they thought, about forty Indians coming towards Hampton with five or six canoes on their heads. Having discovered them the messengers quickly retraced their steps and gave the alarm at Hampton. Henry Dow, one of the town committee, immediately wrote and sent a letter to Salisbury, conveying the intelligence to Major Robert Pike, who commanded the militia of the county of Norfolk. Major Pike, having added a hasty note, forwarded the letter to Mr. Saltonstall, one of the magistrates, who was then at Ipswich on 'court service,' and by him it was sent to the governor. The next morning, September 30, a company of men from Hampton hastened to the scene of carnage, where they met Capt. John Pickering with a company from Portsmouth. The enemy had gone. They were probably preparing to embark at the time they were discovered at Ragged Neck the evening before. Their tracks were traced in the sand, as were also the tracks of two women and one child, whom, with others, it is supposed they carried in captivity. The companies found the dead bodies of ten persons, and thought from what they found in the ashes that three had been burned with the one house. Seven others were missing. The whole loss was twenty persons.

"It is said there were two of the Brackett children carried off by the Indians. One of them, a girl, finally reached Canada, and after she grew up and was married there she came back to Rye and claimed a portion of her father's estate. She took a part of the cattle and a piece of the land was sold to pay her off. It contained about seven acres; Jonathan Locke lived on it, and perhaps bought it; then Richard Lang, and later Samuel A. Trefethen. One of the Bracketts made up quite a number of verses about the woman coming back after her patrimony, which Thomas J. Parsons in his youthful days heard repeated. The brains of one or more children, too young to be easily carried into captivity, were dashed out against a large rock which stood on what is now Wallis road, near Brackett road. This rock, which tradition says bore the stains of blood for many years, was long ago removed in improving the highway. Thomas Walford was mortally wounded on the hill on Brackett road. After he was shot he crawled on his hands and knees to the house of a family named Foss, whose members had either fled to the woods or been massacred by the savages, and drank from a pail of swill he found on the kitchen floor. The hill was called Walford's hill for many years."

Then again Parson writes of the Indian incidents: "With the first settlement of Sandy Beach a garrison house was built, as a matter of course, and was probably located on or near the present Washington road, not far from the seashore.

"It is tradition that at this garrison house the settlers had a 'blunderbuss,' or large gun, which they fired to frighten the Indians; but as powder was very precious in those days it is not probable that it was very often fired for this purpose, unless hostile Indians were known or believed to be in the vicinity. There are writings that show that the Sandy Beach garrison house had some kind of a gun much larger than was ordinarily found in such strongholds. When a settlement was made at Joslyn's (later Locke's) Neck, it was found that one of a number of tall trees there, from the branches of which a view could be had of the Sandy Beach location, had been worn very smooth, supposedly by the climbing up of Indians to watch the garrison house and see when people left it and where they went."

The Locke family featured time and time again in the history of Sandy Beach. There was "John Locke, who settled at Joslyn's Neck, which thereafter for more than two hundred years was known as Locke's Neck, was noted among the Indians for the daring and success with which he fought them, and was correspondingly hated by them in consequence. A raiding party of the savages from the eastward landed one night at the Neck, concealed their canoes in the bushes, and proceeded inland to some point that had been selected to be attacked. Going into the bushes Sunday morning to read his Bible in solitude, Locke discovered the canoes, and immediately cut generous gashes in them with his knife, in places where the cuts would not be seen at a glance. The Indians, on arriving back at the place where they had left their canoes, after their murderous expedition, found the canoes apparently all right, not discovering in the darkness that they had been tampered with; but as soon as they put off from the shore, the canoes took in water so fast that they were compelled to hurriedly land again, and finding the canoes damaged beyond repair the savages were obliged to make their way eastward by land, suffering many hardships and losing several members of their party on the way. Afterwards a party came from the eastward with the express purpose of killing Locke, and surprised him as he was reaping grain in his field, his gun being some distance away, standing against a rock. Securing possession of his gun they shot him through the thighs, and he fell prostrate, but as the savages ran up to tomahawk and scalp him he struck at one of them with his sickle, and cut off the savage's nose. This Indian, it is said, was seen in Portsmouth several times, years later, after trouble with the Indians had ceased in this section, and it was from his account of the manner in which he received his mutilation that the circumstances of Locke's last fight with the Indians were learned. The date of Locke's death was August 6, 1694.

"Jonathan Locke, a grandson of John Locke of Locke's Neck, was born in 1720, and lived in a house built by himself on what is now Washington road, near the Center. One day,

seeing an Indian not very far from the house, he raised the
window in the westerly end a little way, propped it up by
putting a hymn book under it, rested his musket on the
window sill, took careful aim and shot the red man dead. On
being accused by one of his neighbors with killing an Indian
in time of peace he replied that the Indians killed his grandfather, and he would kill an Indian whenever he had
a chance."

As the colonists increased in number they moved from one
locality or another in the territory around the vicinity of
Sandy Beach, ever acquiring and cultivating new land. "The
Berry family went to Farmington, Strafford, and Greenland;
Caswells to Candia. The Foss family to Rochester, Exeter,
Epsom, Greenland, and Barrington; Daltons to Deerfield;
Dolbeers to Epsom; Downs to Wolfeborough; Hobbs to
Epping. The Jenness family to Deerfield, Rochester, Pittsfield,
Epping, and Canaan; Lockes to Epsom, Hampton, Barrington,
Chichester, Chester, and Loudon; Perkins to Meredith;
Philbricks to Epsom. The Randalls to Chester, Deerfield and
Moultonborough; Rands to Epsom, Greenland, Warner,
Gilmanton, and Tuftonborough; Seaveys to Barrington,
Chichester, Rochester, Deerfield, and Greenland; Saunders to
Derry, Epsom, Ossipee, and Chichester; Towles to Epsom
and Epping; Trefethens to Barnstead and Kittery, Maine;
Websters to Epsom and Chester."

Early American lighthouses played a great part in the lives
of these early colonists living along this Strawberry Bank.
During the Revolutionary War to gain control of the coastal
lighthouses was part of military strategy. To be able to
wreck the incoming British men-of-war by blacking out the
lights was a heroic feat for the scheming Yankee. Not only
in wartime were these essential but especially in the daily work

of trading ships going and coming from Europe. Trading companies could not afford to lose men, ships, and cargoes upon the hidden rocks and reefs so the lighthouses were built along the coast. The channels of our harbors would have been of no service whatsoever and the size of the vessels as they improved with use from year to year presented an everchanging problem for those who were signaling.

No one knows exactly when the first lighthouse was built in the world. But we do know that the first means of sending signals from tribe to tribe was by means of building huge bonfires near the shore line and lighting up the way for the boats to ceme in. Then they built these fires higher and up a little higher each time so that they could be seen further and further out in the sea until finally someone, a little more observing than the others, built a permanent mound of stone upon which the fire could rest and the light could be seen at all times from the same level.

Boston Harbor had the most shipping to contend with along the shore and the first American lighthouse was built there to protect the shipping. This lighthouse was lit on September 17, 1716 and vessels coming into Boston Harbor had to pay "a tax of one penny a ton, and another penny for passing outward bound. The coasting vessels were on a different basis, and were obliged to pay two shillings each before clearing the harbor. All fishing vessels, of which there was a great fleet, were taxed five shillings each by the year."

In 1789 the lighthouse at Portsmouth Harbor was built. This was first owned by the New Hampshire colonists and erected through their donations. Then in the same year the Government took over the current expenses of the maintenance of the lighthouse. At this time the Government had control over eight lighthouses along the coast. By doing this the

Government maintained a unity in rescue work and protection against attack from outside sources. It also employed the use of light ships, buoys and other warning signals to lead the ships in and out in safety.

This Whaleback is a wave-swept lighthouse. A wave-swept lighthouse is so constructed that it can withstand the roughest weather and is built, as a rule, out upon a ledge or rock into the sea; for in order to guide the ships in among the shoals or rocky shore or hidden reefs the light had to be placed out in the midst of them. These are able to stand up against the forces of a fierce hurricane and the probable strength of each lighthouse is carefully calculated before it is erected. The top of the lighthouse is built round so that the wind will not become too strong against it and the surface of the walls is smooth so that there will be good resistance against the water. The height of a lighthouse is mathematically reasoned in accordance with the strength of the waves that play about it.

Wood was burned at first for these lights, then coal, oil, and now electricity. The early lamps burned oil and were placed inside of large wooden frames with "thick panes of glass." After these lantern styled lights, came the reflector and the use of the magnifying lens with lights circling about the towers. Many used red and white lights for signaling and throughout the long nights I could always see the flashes of red and white streaking the dark sky.

My Grandfather Caswell, a native of Gosport, Isles of Shoals, had a large ship and brought fish to Portsmouth and shipped them off at the spring markets. Years later he went into Government service and became keeper of the Whaleback lighthouse. Seven years later he ran a retail fish business in Portsmouth and died at the age of eighty-four years.

I would often go when I was young and see the White

Island Lighthouse on the Shoals. From time to time the members of my family either helped or took care of it. My brother Alexander tended the lighthouse for several years. It has a huge revolving light eighty-seven feet above water and is visible fifteen miles away. On clear days it may be seen from Hampton Beach standing forth like a white soldier wrapped in blue. It has saved many lives and no one can ever realize what a lighthouse means to the man at sea when after a weary homeward trip from fishing out on the ocean, you come in through the thick blackness and catch the gleam of that light calling you forth to safety and home. To us Shoalers, that lighthouse was next to our Church. It was the salvation of our souls when coming in through the rough waters with the rain slashing our weather-beaten faces and the wind tossing us about like boards upon the water, we had only to look forward to meeting the light to guide us and greet us in toward shore.

CHAPTER XIX

THERE can be no seacoast with such a crowning floral border as that of New Hampshire in May; when I drive along over the old roads, I see hugging almost every house, clusters and clusters of lilac trees. Their large purple hue tops the brilliant green of their leaves, and scents the whole sea air with a perfume that stifles out the odor of the salt breeze. You may visit New Hampshire any other time of the year, but, to really see New Hampshire in her natural setting is to tour her in the month of May — along the waysides, midst the pines, about the houses, — on every hand is the lilac tree.

Early settlers of Portsmouth came not only with new families and new ideas but also with new plants. Many came with memories of what they had seen in their own country and not forgetting them, hoped to return after them in time to come when they themselves would be rich enough to commandeer their own sailing vessels. Soon, through their industry and good fortune, their sons mastered their own vessels and sailed to many ports on the high seas. Long trips were customary, and practically all points of Europe were touched by these daring men who traded in their fish to bring home presents of silk and finery as well as those things which they had cherished most. Many of these had strange and unbelievable adventures; many of these brought in strange animals and new ways of living in comfort and many returned home as Princes laden down with bounty. Large mansions were built and sailing vessels of the best

[144]

of wood were fashioned. Royalty became the ordinary thing and class strata began to flourish.

These early Yankee shipmasters had many connections with the famous rulers and official diplomats of Europe. There is the story of a Captain Charles Coffin who was a shipmaster in Portsmouth and who had sailed many a ship and cargo to Russia. He did a pretty thriving business and had in his home a family of negro servants. Tobey, the negro husband, was a good-natured, grinning soul who readily made friends with everyone. The Captain, being short of a helper, took Tobey on a voyage to Russia in his large sailing vessel. He had on board a shipment of goods that was to be delivered to the Czar personally. Arriving in Russia, Captain Coffin with his servant, Tobey, became the center of attraction as neither the Czar nor the Russians had seen a negro before. They were amazed at his color, his huge bulk and his pearly, grinning white teeth. The Czar asked for Tobey as a gift, and, after much hackling and arguing, the Captain finally agreed. Tobey was left to the mercy of the Russian court.

Some time passed. Portsmouth had almost forgotten about Tobey, when, suddenly, as if out of a clear sky, the Captain, who was busy loading his ship, was startled by a voice immediately behind him, "Hallo, Cap'n Coffin, here I is afer m'wife n'chillun."

The Captain looked up and there in front of him gleefully grinning, was Tobey dressed to kill. The Czar had made him an official of the court, and had dressed him up in a bright uniform covered with gold braid. He wore a huge diamond ring which they had presented him. He had had a grand time. He enjoyed living in Russia and was going to return right away on the next ship going out. He bought his wife and children and returned to Russia and was heard of no more.

It was a Yankee shipmaster who brought over the linden tree from England and planted it in front of the Wentworth-Gardner House. It stands like a huge sentinel with overladen arms in the front yard. This Wentworth-Gardner House was built in 1760 by Mark Hunking Wentworth and was given by him to his son Thomas. It is an old colonial homestead and the materials for its building were shipped directly from England. The face of the reigning Queen of England of that day is said to be carved in the key of the window arch. The skilled ship carvers on the shore cut out most of the carvings and a remarkable job it was, with such tools as they had to work with in those days. It is now owned by the New York Metropolitan Museum and contains many antiques and portraits besides its sample of Georgian architecture. Mildred Haley O'Brien, a direct descendant of the famous Samuel Haley of the Shoals, is now caretaker and hundreds of tourists visit the House during the year.

I was a young boy when Captain Charles Drowne owned it. My father, after he had moved in to the Mainland, rented the house from him, and our family lived there for quite a spell. We children delighted in running up and down the famous staircase and playing about the fireplace. The spinning attic with its walls of Indian red fascinated us and at that time the back section had not been added on and there was a larger back yard. It was an airy place and well suited for our large family. This Captain Drowne was a good sailor, and on August 27, 1891, he won the regatta at the Piscataqua Yacht Club being master of the schooner "Tryphose," and Captain T. O. Marvin being master of the "Sagamore." This was in the same year that my uncle, Captain Levi W. Downs, took over the schooner "Grace Choate," becoming master in place of Captain Edward Robinson. Little did we think then that people would have to pay admission to the home where we played about so simply and naturally. The Old Linden Tree watches the changes; looks up over the Old River as she moves along, and says nothing.

The linden tree came from England, but from the far off land of Tibet, from the mountain regions of Asia, over trail, by camel, by ship, came the beautiful lilac. Governor Benning Wentworth, in and about 1740 or so, wanted a beautiful and hardy tree with flowers to place about his new home on Little Harbor Road. Through some mysterious channel and foresight, or that piercing ingenuity which most of the Governors possessed at that time, he got hold of the lilac tree. Realizing the beauty and rarity of the tree, he planted it upon three sides of his home. Now the old Wentworth place on Little Harbor Road is still there with its sturdy twisted trees. John Templeton Coolidge is the owner. From this spot, the lilac is supposed to have spread over America, going westward with each new covered wagon, southward with each new slave ship; and north with each French and Indian battle. As I travel over the roads through Boston and the New England States I see every now and then a lilac tree blooming in May; I feel a thrill of pride in knowing that that tree is an off-shoot and in some way, at some time, sprouted from the same salt air as I.

Of all the holidays in Portsmouth, Memorial Day is the most important one. It has always been the day when we seafaring folk have placed the lilac on an altar of reverence and worshipped it. Many a time as I have walked the streets just before Memorial Day, I have heard the children say to one another:

"I hope the lilacs won't be dead before we have Memorial Day."

Years ago every father of us took great pride in dressing

our children up in brand new white clothes so that they might look their best to march in the parade on Memorial Day. The clothes would be laid out weeks ahead and the children could not seem to wait for the day to come. When it did come, what a time! What a bustle of excitement! Everyone had to be ready and on time to be in the parade.

It was a beautiful sight to see those children marching down the street. Fifty or more children, of all sizes and ages, stiffly dressed in white, moved slowly down to the Old South Mill Bridge with large bouquets of purple and white lilacs in their tiny arms. As each group reached the bridge they threw over their bouquets into the river—just bunches and bunches of lilacs. The muggy colored green of the river became transformed into a blanket of purple and white forming, as the lilacs wended their way downstream with the current, magical pictures of design floating out to sea. These children were proud. They had dutifully commemorated those whose lives had been lost in the work of the sea. And turning about, we all went to the Old South Cemetery to commemorate our graves with vases of lilacs. Memorial Day was always a busy and important day.

The lilac is Portsmouth's own flower as well as being that of the State of New Hampshire. The State Government voted on March 28, 1919, that the lilac should become the official flower of the State of New Hampshire, but it was long before recognized by the people of Portsmouth. It flourished there. One reason for the tree to do so well in and about us is the fact that our climate is well suited to its growth. As it is supposed to have come down from a vigorous rigid climate, so our weather here, with its strong winds and its salt moist air, dry summer days and the strong invigorating rays of the sun, help to make it bloom in hardy fashion. Once rooted in the ground, the lilac tree withstands the fiercest gales and lives throughout the winter to shine forth each May.

A ship brought over the first linden tree and a ship brought over the first lilac tree. Ships that sailed from way over the ocean, handmade ships that braved the storms and hardships, to bring back comforts and luxuries. Ships mastered by men who by their persistence and daring made our lulls from distress and worry, happy in a beautiful setting. How fortunate was the State of New Hampshire to have men such as these to master the seas!

CHAPTER XX

A S WE PLANT life's footsteps on the shores of memory, our later tracks seem to travel on much more swiftly in the panorama of time. Events crowd one upon the other and seem to blend in an endless stream of recordings losing their vividness in their multiplicity of facts. The ideals become realities and the urge to accomplish lessens with the oncoming of life's endings. Politics, domestic happenings and the everyday toil register notes of despair and happiness; shaping views that are so different and so much wiser than those of youth and early manhood.

I was not a fishing man all of my life. I did and took part in many other works and activities. At one time I was a pilot between Portsmouth and Boston. For four summers I was captain of the "Alvin Fuller" of Boston, a pleasure yacht, from the years 1909 to 1912. We would cross along the coast to the Marion coast all summer so that in the fall of 1912 I brought the boat back to Boston and Mr. Fuller sold it to Boston port yard.

Every now and then, I have delved into the intricacities of public affairs—perhaps not on a major scale, but in that everyday smattering of a layman interested in the well being of his community and state. I joined the Fire Department as a call man—a minute man at the sudden ring. I became interested and worked for advancement. For ten years I was a member of the William I. Sampson hook and ladder and then I became the chief. Being chief was difficult as it took up so much of my time so after having been twenty-seven years in the Fire Department I retired. A short while after my retirement,

representatives came to see me and asked me to be the head
of the Department but as I was getting on in years, I thanked
them and declined the offer, although I would have liked to
have accepted as it was considered to be an honor.

Forty years and more of my life were spent in being interested and following along in the strategies of polities. Politics
is a fascinating and wary game if you only know how to play
it without letting the other fellow know much about anything.
I have helped to put many a man into office. There was one
great man whom I always admired for his wonderful tact
and smooth friendliness in his political dealing. That was
Lawyer Guptil who was one of the finest politicians that
Portsmouth has ever known. Whenever he spoke or moved,
he would be able to have worthwhile influence over the feelings and sympathies of the citizens. Being his right hand
man, I shared in many of his policies. He has since passed
away and like all good men, we, in Portsmouth, have missed
his wise council and shrewd advice. Portsmouth, to my mind,
has never had another one like him since.

I remember well the day that President Garfield was shot.
It happened during the summer months. All the steamers
came out that day with their flags at half mast. This was the
year of the yellow dust, or yellow day as it has been called.
Another President who has always stood foremost in my mind
was Teddy Roosevelt, the wielder of the big stick policy. It
was during his term that I delved more deeply into the realms
of politics in and around the year 1905. He was certainly a
powerful man. As one of the ardent followers of the Bull
Moose party I worked extensively for the party during his
administration. I ran on the ticket for office in the city government but lost in the recount by only one under. As a
member of the Republican party, I served on the Board of
Registrars for five years and held the office of Selectman for

another five years. I was not an office seeker for my manager wanted me to work on the outside ring of the party. He remarked to me: "If you get into office, they soon forget you."

Time traveled on. My wife and I watched continuously the children go and come from the old Haven School. The children prancing past our door called us Grandpa and Grandma because we were the oldest around there. For thirty years we lived in the same house which is about two hundred years old with the same doors and the same latch still remaining. I would never change things like these.

I could go on and write of the events that happened in the past. I was always looking ahead but I did not get up to where I had dreamed to be but I got along all right but that was not my will; I wanted to go higher and higher, yet, I lived, and lived all the same. We have to work harder now to keep up with the times and now it is getting over the sensation, so laden with thoughts of grief, that my father and mother have gone and also my wife. It leaves me to remain to think over of what stuff life is made.

At the age of seventy-one, I have just been appointed Harbor Master of the Piscataqua Harbor, in Portsmouth. This was indeed most pleasant, as I have held and still hold a most deep admiration for the whirling blue-green eddies of the swift river. There is no such river as this in the whole wide world. None can equal its magic spell that it holds over me. I have been placed in charge of the one place I treasured most. Ever since I began to reason I have been in and out of this Harbor. To be Harbor Master is really an important matter.

Sometimes it is not the amount of the salary offered; it is the prestige that such an office holds its appeal. For instance, I have been made an honorable member of the Portsmouth Yacht Club, and a special member of the Portsmouth police force to look after the affairs of the water front. There are any number of boats moored and drawn up along the river front which have to be protected from wrongdoers and damage by the mischievous hands of playing children. Everyday there will be someone who will come to me to tell that their boat has been lost over night. It is up to me then, to get in touch with the people all along the waterfront to find out if there were any witnesses to the stealing of it, the boat having accidentally slipped its moorings has been seen out in the deep by the early morning fishermen, or as in some cases, the real culprit is found out and I have to report him to headquarters.

The job of the Harbor Master is to keep the channel clear. Any vessels that are coming into harbor to anchor are supposed to keep the channel open and not to block it. Many of these ships coming up the river will often keep going back and forth looking for a place to anchor, it is the Harbor Master's duty to see that they have safe anchorage. If any ship is in distress it must be aided in every way possible. Many times as there are road hogs on the roads so on the river, there are river hogs, those owners of ships who will take another company's anchoring spot, or who will without leave, anchor theirs in the same spot. The Harbor Master has to straighten out many interesting and hot disputes upon this question. It is also his duty to see that no one dumps rubbish so that it will tend to fill up spots on the channel and to keep the general aspect of the banks of decent morale. I am very proud in my own heart to think that after all these years of hardships I have been made the master of the river that I have treasured all my life even though it may be for only a short period.

Thus, approaching life's safe harbor, my sailing has not been smooth and has not been too rough, for I have dipped from the crest of the salty waves to the hollow depths, feeling the sprays of salt being whipped into my memory and smattering my skin with the cracking salt of sharp incidents, with the sunshine of honest achievement healing their wounds with its violet ray of satisfaction in having had a bout with life.

CHAPTER XXI

TIDES OF DEFENSE

WHIRS AND WHIRS of airplanes over my head, ceremonial splashes of newly made submarines, Coast Guard Cutters, heavy-laden freighters chugging and steaming, gloomy gray shadows of destroyers out at sea, passport inspections, dim-outs, black-outs, guards of patrols, blinking of signals, mysteries of radio beams streaking the fogs, air-raid warnings' wailings at practice, Red Cross ambulances and canteen units whizzing past in frequent drills, O. P.A.'s, W. P. I.'s, rationing books, seem to have blown in like a north easter, twirling around and around our civilian life and bringing to us the fact that to be of use to one's country is to be of service to all. No matter how small a man may be, to be able to take part in the serving of his country is to puff him up into the Big Shot he had always hoped to become.

Just the Second World War! The fish are beginning to find shelter from the blasting horrors of the sea in toward the shores again. The Isles of Shoals have been taken entirely into government custody, the clouds rising up over the lighthouse have become sinister in their forebodings and the skies have a gloomy reflection of the red of battle fronts far away. Our old familiar streets are becoming bare of customary young passers-by and the hum and stress of the reverberations of common living have quieted down while it gains a speed of momentum that is patriotically beneficial in its vortex. I had never once dreamed that I would have a son in the service or that my other son's wife would publicly, in the theatre I often attended, be presented a bouquet of Mrs.

Miniver's roses for having five sons serving in various quarters of the world. Never, thought I, would I ever be out pulling in my lobster traps alone again; yet, so have I, my other sons are doing defense work on the Navy Yard. So busy have I become. My work as Harbor Master, as Port Warden and as a member of the State Special Police take up all of my idle moments. Letters keep coming in from Washington with directions, restrictions, and orders and very often I have helped the Coast Guardsmen in their work. Reports have to be made on the clearing of the harbors for the navigation of the vessels coming in and going out, the thickness of the ice during the winter months, and so many other details have kept my mind occupied with the safety along the old river which has meant so much to me. Little did I ever believe that I would cooperate in keeping the channels of New England open for emergency sailings. I have not had a chance to feel old.

It is a great feeling to know that you are able to do it and that every thing is being carried on in our country in the same democratic way. When I was a young fellow and used to see the old people working, I thought it was a sin—so old and to be working. Now I am seventy-three years old and am beginning to wonder if the youngsters think that of me. Way back in those days a man was good as long as he could work; but of late years a man has become considered done at the age of forty, and now again the time is returning when one is as good as the other according to the work he accomplishes. We have all, today, young and old, the opportunity to do our part. We shouldn't let anything get by us at this time of trouble as Our Master says there is a job to do and we are all going to do it right the same and will know about it when we are all over it. We are all working feverishly in the dark just now but the sun will shine on some day, good and bright. I trust we are the people of hope and in that way we shall be able to stand together always.

Defense measures along our shorelines have slowed down the number of visitors and transients that used to throng through the city. The thousands of teachers, travelers, artists, authors, and students who would at one time be streaming continuously by, visiting landmarks and museum, painting sky and outline, have become few in number. Now the city teems with defense workers, soldiers, sailors, marines, and of course the women's army, the Waacs, the Waves, the Spars. Yet, this year we carried on our city election in the same manner as always and as if nothing unusual were happening about us. The people have their minds set and they are determined to carry on their common habits in their own individual ways and abide by the rules of rightful living that they have been accustomed to. The changes are only temporary until our victory has been won. It is great to realize that we live in such an energetic country at this time of trouble. It is sometimes trying to suppress our thoughts as for our own safety, our lips have become sealed but some day in the future we are going to holler it out and talk it off in the good old Yankee way.

I have had to give up much of my fishing grounds as the army has taken much of it over in order to mine it to protect the harbor. This means sacrificing in a small way which amounts to so little in comparison with those who are not only sacrificing their fortunes, but also their blood. A fisherman never actually gets through with his work no matter what the odds. He has a job of his very own. He has not the time to clutter up his mind with pretty thoughts but must continually bend it to his work. So a real fisherman seldom gets to wearing a white collar and sitting at his desk with the fragrance of roses about him. His means are his big rubber boots standing midst the aroma of fresh smelling fish with his weather eye watching for the fish to blow in. Even during wars he has to keep wearing his boots for the army and civilians have to eat and this is a part of the nation's food supply. Even though a fisherman makes one catch of even smelts a day; he is doing his job. As the farmer, he is an essential war worker although his dangers are far more numerous. Mines or submarines may unexpectedly be lurking about his catch or as in the cases of fishermen working along the shores of Europe he may be strafed by bombers or blown to death. The hardy fishermen of England have shown their grit in bringing in their catch and in rescue work along the coasts, unafraid of weather or bestial inhumanity. We are their descendants and their allies; we, if the occasion should ever strike, can and will do likewise.

Along our coasts the first European landed. It was here bands after bands of Indians were fought off. Here the American Revolutionists took their stand against the English Tories. John Paul Jones set out from these shores to chase the British frigates back to England. The most able and noted leaders and statesmen during the Civil War raised their voices from these shore lines. The Spanish prisoners were housed among us. The Russo-Japanese treaty was signed at the Navy Yard. Indeed, men of valor and ambition arose from the seamen's ranks at all times to offer their services to their country. It is not unusual then, that at this time, the boys pouring from the banks of the Atlantic will once again prove to be among the foremost to dare and to gain recognition among the armed forces.

As I watch these boys leave one by one from our city's streets, as I observe civilians drilling in the pitch blackness of preparedness manoeuvers, and as I look out over the horizons of what may be tomorrow, a feeling of awe and reverence comes over me—a feeling of the minuteness of man and the immensity of the universe.

CHAPTER XXII

SPRAYS OF SALT

GLIDING into Life's harbor with full rigging and very few repairs after having sailed through the river rights of living is a gratifying sail. You just sit and wonder how the sprays of salt have washed over you and yours over and over again; and, have yet left you sailing along. Time, work, and money, have faded from your deck and only that spirit of satisfaction plays upon your memory. Life's span is short and the shores are forever changing, leaving everything or nothing in its carving, pebbles, stones, boulders of despair have been eroded away while the sands of time have slipped quietly away never to be used again.

Tranquil thoughts as these must pass through the minds of every old Shoaler, as he stands on the mainland and looks over toward the rocks that were once his home. The Shoalers who have really loved and revered these rocks are passing away one by one. There was a time when I used to meet Oscar Laighton on the streets of Portsmouth, and we used to chat congenially about the good old times on the Shoals. The last time that I saw him, he was in a wheel chair but his eyes were still of the twinkling blue with that pleasing smile and his body still held that artistic poise which was so inherent in his family. He died in April in 1939. He lived to a good ripe old age for within a few months he would have lived a hundred years and within his last years, he attended the services held at Star, delighting in playing his puns and joking with the visitors. He loathed to leave the Isles where he had spent the better days of his life so he had his body cremated and his ashes strewn ceremoniously over the Islands. Ashes that rightfully blended with the dust of the rocks and the salt of the sea.

There was poor old Wilbert Haley who was accidentally drowned when he became entangled in some rope near Union Wharf at the age of seventy. He was one who earned his early living from fishing and in his later years he had been working at the Oceanic Hotel on Star Island. He was a good soul, individualistic and self-demanding, and it seems sad that he met his end this way.

My brother Edward Sargent passed away in June 1940. He was building inspector of Portsmouth at the time he died at the age of seventy-four. During his early life, as I, he followed the sea. Then becoming interested in my Uncle Oliver's meat and fish market he remained there for fifty years. At the time of my Uncle Oliver's death, he became the sole owner of the business and carried it on until he retired a few years ago. He was very active in the affairs of the Republican Party and he served in many offices of the city. He represented Ward 5 in the State Legislature in 1917 in which he recommended most ardently the building of the Memorial Bridge which was later finished in 1923. And at about that time he served on the Alderman Council. He was a member of many lodges and chapters of the various clubs and was a high Free Mason. Up to his last days he and I would meet in his office and discuss old affairs of our childhood and play a game or so of cards. Energetic and ambitious to the last hour, he displayed the agility which is so notable in any old Shoaler.

The love for these Isles is bred in you. I have traveled from them and when not on them or on the ocean about them; I am lost even though I live only a short distance away. I take my car, drive down to the beach and see the shape of the Isles rising out of the sea—like a mirage in the haze. I like to park and watch the boats as they go about their daily tasks and my own boat with my son taking over is among them. I look and wonder how I stood and did it for so many years. It was a life worth having—an independent one—no one to trouble or to boss you about. There were no opening whistles and no closing sirens, you could go out when you felt like it and stay as long as you wanted to. It was a task to be enjoyed, not one to be regimented,

The Real Old Shoalers who fostered me when I was a child and who so gracefully overlooked my minor mistakes, my mother whose love of cooking so whetted my appetite to the extremes of gluttony, my wife who so fondly shared with me my sorrows and joys, and my children and their children who have gone out into other lanes in their pursuit of happiness, will always remain as glowing landmarks in my memory. Fishing out of the deep, working to become someone respected and appreciated have edged on my course and steered it through many a whirlpool of criticism and sound judgment. That ability and knowledge that I am useful in my daily tasks to the good of the community in my position as Harbor Master is comforting to my worth. Not that I have become laden with age, but the gratifying load of pleasant thoughts that surround me have lightened the pathway for me.

I have seen some pretty hard times on that old ocean but I never was afraid. I have been shipwrecked, I have been broken down, and have laid for hours waiting for someone to come to get me; and, they always did. I have fallen over-board into the ocean; but I was saved. So what had I to be afraid of. I always knew that when my time came, no matter where I was, I would go as others had before me.

Thus I wait in the harbor of life, facing the salt breezes as they blow my way wondering whether today or tomorrow or the next will brush my sprays of salt to the winds of eternity.

CHAPTER XXIII

MY BROTHER OREN

A S I, my brother Oren, has lived a long time weathering fog and sunshine of gaining a living out of the ocean. For eighty years he has been about these shores. With his quiet smile and his ruddy curly hair he could be seen at any time in the early nineteen hundreds cutting fish along the wharves. To him, as to me, the old ocean has meant his tie on life, and no matter where he has traveled, from his winters in Florida and his stays in the White Mountains, he has always returned for that inevitable longing of the crisp salt air and the familiar sounds of the fog horns in the distance.

His story as he tells it in his own words in his own quiet, terse manner is as he told me:

"I was born on the Isles of Shoals in 1863. I don't remember much about the very first years of my life. I remember my Grandmother saying to me at one time that when she first went on the Isles of Shoals, she had to go over to Hog Island to get huckleberries for fuel for there was no means of getting any over from the Mainland. As a youngster the coming and going of the boarders at the Hotels was my means of earning a few pennies. I would string shells and sell them for from twenty-five to fifty cents apiece to the boarders. They were always very kind to me and always paid me well. I would row them from one Island to another, many of them being artists and authors. I used to get paid for showing where Miss Underhill's chair was and for telling over and over again her story. Often there would be as many as seven to eight hundred boarders gathered on the Islands.

The prize fights were of great interest to me. Great, big prize fights would be held in a ring on Smutty Nose Island. They were professionals. Two large steamboats would bring them down from Boston and crowds of people would come over from the Mainland to see them.

"I first sailed out to sea on an old Irish Boat, the 'St. Peters.' We did some fishing in her. After this trip I joined up under Ed Jameson and sailed with him on the 'Jennie Lee.' Forty years ago I did a great deal of mackerel fishing in and out of Dorchester Bay. Later I went to Boston on the 'Champion' to Swampscot Bay. At one time I was ship-wrecked on the Middle Shoals in Boston Harbor. I went back to Gloucester and from there sailed back on the 'Flying Cloud' to the Grand Banks. We returned to Gloucester with the catch and sailed on the 'Joseph O. Proctor' on which trip I was stranded on Sandy Point. From there I sailed up through Guttacancer and up to Cape Knoll from which point we got bait to go fishing and started for the Green Banks. We steered on to the left of Cape Knoll in the night under double reef sails and just cleared the 'Madalene' and were saved.

"When bound home from the Green Banks we made the Sable Islands in five fathoms of water fifteen miles on the New England end of it. We made Cape Cod in six or seven days from the Banks to Gloucester. I made another trip on the 'Flying Cloud,' and another on the 'Mary R. Clark' from Beverly. Later I went down to the Banks again, down through Great Brittain to Bergen's Rock and came home from the trip with the Greenland Expedition vessey 'Beni Whaler' with Captain Woodbury. On the 'Mary E. Caswell' I went fishing down East after having left Captain Woodbury, as the 'Mary E. Caswell' was the ship of my Uncle Oren Caswell.

On the way home we were shipwrecked on the rocks of Wells Bay or Wells Rock. The ship foundered and I had to jump overboard off the main boom in the dory and got ashore. I finally made shore soaking wet and very tired. The people near the shore greeted us and treated us very kindly. They offered us good clean beds, good clothing, and plenty to eat. A tugboat came to get us and took us back to Portsmouth. Then I went off to Newburyport and sailed under Captain Green and stayed and worked for a while codfishing off the coast. I sailed quite a bit on the 'Albert Woodbury' and the 'Agnes E. Downs' with my Uncle Levi Downs. These two vessels were built up East and I went down and helped fit out the 'Agnes E. Downs' and went sailing with Uncle Levi out mackereling. Many is the ship I've sailed in, from time to time. I went under a fellow named Julius Englebristen, went trawling in a vessel named the 'Cecelia' and set out again with Oren Caswell in the 'Norman'.

"I've tried my hand at all kinds of fishing off the New England Coast, but the fishing that comes first to my mind is the fishing for the ground sharks on the Grand Banks. In the old sailing vessels we used to set our trawls for the ground shark or the nurse fish as we often called them. The meat or the skin of these fish wasn't any good, we only caught them for the liver. Their lives were used to make machine oil. The largest one we ever caught was one weighing a little over a thousand pounds. There would be about one hundred and fifty pounds of liver in one of them. We would cut the liver up into pieces and place them in barrels where we would let them stay until they formed the oil. They netted us from seventy-five to eighty cents a bucket. These fish were not dangerous to catch for they were numb fish. We caught them by trawls. They would get snarled up in the trawls and then we would pull them in. Their skin was as rough as sandpaper and very often they could free themselves by cutting the lines but more often they were hauled in before they had a chance. Sometimes we would mix this liver with cod liver to make a new mixed oil to be used for machines. Many of us earned a good living from catching these ground sharks.

"There were many other things in my life besides fishing. I attended Haven School in the years about 1877. Then I was married in 1885 and reared twelve children, of whom five passed away. One child was instantly killed by being run over by Frank Jones's Brewery truck and two passed away with black diphtheria. One son served in the United States Cavalry in the First World War, and another has served as a prominent member of politics in the Concord State House of New Hampshire, for the last several years. All of my sons have done well and are all now engaged in essential war work, one as leading man on the Navy Yard, and another is doing photographic work in defense industries. I am proud of every one of them; for even my youngest is buying up property along the water front.

"As I grew older I started lobstering, which I soon gave up to work with Captain Edward Jameson doing lobstering handling for six years. I left there and went back to lobstering again. Then I went out cutting fish up for the Eldrich Portsmouth Market. After working there a few years I went to work on the City and remained on there for twenty years. While working on the City I was accidentally stamped on by a horse, my face was badly cut and my ankle cut in two. For eight weeks I didn't work but went right back again when I was well. Three years later I was struck by an automobile and my left leg was smashed and cut up. I left the City when well over seventy years of ago and went back to lostering off and on from then on. Now I have retired for a while from active fishing until I feel that urge again.

"I have traveled somewhat. I have spent a few winters down in Florida, some time in the White Mountains, and some time in Nova Scotia, besides the very many sea trips I have taken up and down the coast of New England. Yet I still prefer my chair at my window on South Mill Street that overlooks the South Mill Bridge and looks across at Pierce's Island and the Navy Yard, and I often sit there and dream of the times that used to be when I would see the old white sails of the fishing vessels coming into port and hear the yells of the fishermen as they unloaded their fish ashore. It is indeed a blessing that a man has forever his mind to look into and pass the hours away."

INDEX